Countdown: A Life in 20 Songs

by

Tom Waldman

To Mom,
A journey we
took together...
mostly.
Love,
Tom

Martin Powers Publishing

Bryan, Texas

Countdown: A Life in 20 Songs

First Edition
Published in the United States

Martin Powers Publishing
801 Dellwood St. PMB 357
Bryan, TX 77802

ISBN: 978-0-9838824-5-9

DEDICATION

To Zach and Ethan,
who are extending the Waldman legacy,
in words and music.

ACKNOWLEDGMENTS

I was born in 1956, the same year that rock and roll became the dominant form of American popular music, although it would take a decade for the two of us to get acquainted. I want to first thank Chuck Berry, Fats Domino, Buddy Holly, Jerry Lee Lewis, Elvis Presley, Little Richard, and the early Doo Wop groups, who were making it possible for me to grow up in a world more exciting than the one they left behind.

In September 1966, a few weeks after I turned 10, my younger brother, John, and I watched the debut of a new television program called *The Monkees*. By the time of the closing credits, I was in love with the group. A few months later, I was in love with rock and roll, or if you prefer, rock. Fifty-six years later, my feelings haven't diminished one bit.

Thanks to Mike, Davy, Micky, Peter, John, Paul, George, Ringo, Mick, Keith, Brian, Charlie, Bill, Bob, Smokey, Martha, Berry, Jimi, Aretha, Jack, Pete, Roger (Daltrey), Roger (McGuinn), Jimmy, Robert, John (Fogerty), David, Bruce, Joe, James, Linda, Sly, Brenton, Michael, Madonna, Prince, Belinda, Susanna, Nile, Bernard, Liam, and Noel for bringing such joy into my life these many years. You don't know me, but boy, do I know you.

Special thanks to the guests who appeared on *Rock and Roll Stories*, the program I hosted in Los Angeles from 2013 to 2015. This super group includes Wayne Kramer, Johnny Rivers, Paul Stookey, Charles Wright, Lonnie Jordan, Vicki

Peterson, Little Willie G, Louise Goffin, Eddie Holman, Thomas Dolby, the late B.J. Thomas, Stephen Bishop, and the late P.F. Sloan. There are few things I enjoy more than talking to musicians about music. I will cherish these conversations forever.

If you haven't tried it, I strongly recommend pop music as a way to make friends. I met Jon and Joel Bellman in 1973, and we still talk and occasionally argue about our likes and dislikes to this day. Thanks to the Bellman guys for the late-night record sessions in the mid-70s. Thanks also to Pete Sanders, sometime participant, and head of the eternal Buddy Holly fan club.

In the fall of 1978, David Reyes and I worked together at Tower Records in West Covina, California. We established a close friendship, which then became a partnership that resulted in one magazine article, one book, a three-CD anthology, a documentary film, and a musical. Thank you, David, for the music education and years of creativity.

In 2014, James Holvay, songwriter extraordinaire, appeared as a guest on *Rock and Roll Stories*. The next thing I knew, he had agreed to compose the songs for an original rock and roll musical I had written entitled *Eastside Heartbeats*. Two years later, the show debuted at Casa 0101 Theatre in the Boyle Heights section of Los Angeles. Thank you, James, for helping to take *Heartbeats* from crazy dream to sold-out run.

While I am on the subject of the musical, thanks to my dear friend, Steve Feinberg, a mentor to me and director of the show's second run. Of course, none of it would have happened without Gary St. Germain, our tireless arranger, or the producer, Maria Elena Yepes, who raised the funds when no one else could or would. Thanks to both of you.

Although this book is a very personal reflection, it could not have happened without the generous assistance of others. Thanks to Roger Kempler and Ellen Girardeau Kempler, who read an early draft of the manuscript and offered a slew of invaluable suggestions; Chip Diggins, who persuaded me to ditch the stock political analysis, among other things; Lane Quigley, who caught some embarrassing errors before they became public knowledge; and dear Heather Rothman, an incredible editor, who kept me focused on the task at hand and offered her own critical insights.

The book you see owes great thanks to talented cover art designer Ty Rulli and photographer Lew Groner for their creativity and skills. Credit for chapter artwork is thanks to Turntable Clipart (#298075) and Movie Clipart Transparency (#3060615).

A special thanks to my editor, the amazing Dawn Lee Wakefield, who placed her skills in the service of this book despite having a million other professional and personal responsibilities. "Countdown" would simply not exist in any form without her contributions.

Thanks to my brother, John, for 50+ years of conversations about rock and roll, and for getting *Happy Jack*, *Magical Mystery Tour*, and *Sticky Fingers* as presents. Thanks to my sister, Katy, for bringing country rock into the house.

Finally, thanks to my parents, Ted and Nancy Waldman, for starting us off with classical and jazz, and then making the seamless transition to Simon and Garfunkel, the Mamas and Papas, and the Beatles. I followed your lead.

TABLE OF CONTENTS

INTRODUCTION

From my teenage years into my early 20s, I judged people on their music preferences. I believed that boys, and especially girls, who listened to gentle, mournful pop songs were slaves to their overwrought emotions. I insisted that Elton John fans had no right to also claim an affinity for true rock. I maintained that kids who loved Black Oak Arkansas or Brownsville Station — this was in the early 1970s — had below average intelligence. I argued that devotees of Grand Funk Railroad had never been exposed to actual music.

On the other hand, people who listened to the Rolling Stones—me, for instance—had cool conferred upon them, despite appearances to the contrary. White kids who dug James Brown were superior on every level to white kids who didn't. Girls who were into The Doors or Hendrix were sexier than girls who were into Carole King and looks had nothing to do with it.

I took the position at the time, and still do, that our choices in music say more about us than what films, plays, or television programs we prefer. I had a girlfriend in the early 1980s who was a huge fan of the *Star Wars* franchise, although not at the level of the costumed devotees who wait in line for days. By contrast, I didn't need to see any of the films to feel like a whole person. As a little kid, I had enjoyed monster movies, not so much because of the creatures, but that the military might be deployed in an often vain attempt to defeat them. That was the extent of my interest in the genre that I broadly and probably inaccurately characterized as science fiction.

It mattered little to me that my girlfriend loved *Star Wars* and its immediate successors. The relationship didn't hang in the balance every time she brought up George Lucas or Harrison Ford. I even went with her to see the second film, *The Empire Strikes Back*, which I enjoyed more than I had expected.

But if she had sworn by Kiss, owned records by Journey, or demanded that I accompany her to a Boston concert, it would have precipitated a major crisis. I would have responded with a smart-ass remark, followed by a sarcastic putdown, topped off with an ongoing propaganda campaign, as if I were trying to wean her from a cult. I would have risked the relationship to make my point.

    *   *   *

A few years ago, I wrote two drafts of a memoir based on the idea that I could tell my life story through the events I experienced either directly or indirectly from the beginning of historical consciousness — learning about Pearl Harbor Day as a five-year-old in December 1961 — to the present. As a lifelong history buff, it seemed like both a logical and uncommon approach for a person who was not in any way a historical figure to write his autobiography.

Although I did not lack for examples — assassinations, riots, wars, political scandals, ecological catastrophes — I had great difficulty arriving at a recurring theme. The text jumped from anecdote to anecdote with only the obvious device of advancing chronology as linkage.

I could not work my way out of the problem. Still, writing that memoir was not a colossal waste of time and effort. I discovered something else that led to this book.

In a number of chapters, rock, soul, or funk songs played a significant role, at times edging proper history off the stage. These were not trite exercises in nostalgia, but instances where a particular song defined my place in the world at that moment. The songs I listened to obsessively offered a window into my political, social, cultural, and sexual development. Better yet, music provided the connecting thread that had been missing from the earlier book.

Once I recognized the possibilities, I sat down and wrote a list of songs that have mattered to me — for a variety of reasons — since I first became a rock and roll fanatic in the fall of 1966. I settled on 20; 10 was far too few, and 40, a significant number in pop music, was far too many.

My list includes songs that crept up on me, when I least expected it: songs that protected me from physical or psychic harm; songs that came out of the distant past but pointed toward future opportunities; songs that were put to work in mysterious ways; songs that smacked me on the head, when I needed to wake up; songs that might seem apolitical to you but were purely political to me; songs by artists with short hair and songs by artists with long hair; songs by glittery Brits and songs by manic Yanks; songs on their way out and songs on their way in; songs that were more left than right and songs that were more right than left; and one song that wasn't a song at all, but a cult classic film about an all-female rock group.

Most of the choices on my playlist would not be included among my all-time favorites. Aesthetics were considered, but not to the exclusion of details relevant to this analysis. The songs that made a difference in my life were not always the songs that I liked best, or even liked very much at all. The chapters are chronological, but not the songs; a few from the 1950s showed up in the 1970s, and one from the 1960s made an unexpected appearance in the 2010s.

When I first started listening to pop music in the fall of 1966, I did not dare dream, let alone expect that I would make a modest second career out of rock and roll; two books, a PBS documentary, a television talk show, co-producer of a three-CD anthology, and a musical, for which I wrote the script and most of the song lyrics. I have included on my list a few songs with a direct connection to my extracurricular projects. If it's too much to say rock and roll saved my life, it sure made it more interesting.

This music-as-memoir encompasses my life from the age of 10 to the age of 59, from the Monkees to the Buckinghams, a happy accident that led to the musical. To this day, I continue to talk about the Beatles, Stones, Girl Groups, Motown, and Led Zeppelin with the same fervor as back in 1975. I have read and reread rock memoirs, biographies, and collections of criticism. The subject has influenced my intellectual life as well.

Countdown: A Life in 20 Songs is in one sense the story of life lived with the active participation of dusty 45s, well-played albums, and miraculous CD collections, plus turntables, stereo systems, AM and FM radio, and YouTube. At an earlier time, I carted my collection of vinyl from dorm to dorm, apartment to apartment, house to house, until the physical strain became too much, and I sold it to a record store. But the memories are fond ones.

In another sense, the book is history, politics, gender roles, race, ethnicity, sexuality, feminism, the environment, generational divides, and the grit of Los Angeles told to the beat of rock and roll, soul, disco, and funk. A story of the interplay between music and historical events, music and societal trends, music and personal highs and lows, told by a 65-year-old guy who was lucky to have been alive at a time of extraordinary musical activity and political ferment.

CHAPTER 1

"The Star Spangled Banner," 1814

Jimi Hendrix, 1970

His name was Gus, and we attended the same elementary school in Tempe, Arizona. I was in first grade and he was in either third or fourth. Despite the fact that I was young and short and Gus was old and gigantic, he had acknowledged me from time to time on campus with a nod of the head. I privately called him "Gus Bus" due to his girth. We may have played a few games of playground football with other boys during recess.

It was one evening after dinner, around 7:30, and I swear that the streets were deserted, like the next-to-last scene in a classic western. This large kid emerged down the block and quickly closed the distance between us. "Hi, Tommy," he said, the name by which I went, reluctantly, until the age of nine. "Hi Gus," I responded, cautiously, not quite trusting his ebullient manner. He moved closer, using his enormous size as a means of intimidation. I had never been bullied and didn't recognize the obvious signs. I should have run, very fast, in the opposite direction. But I only realized that later, during my own private debrief.

My patriotic antagonist didn't waste much time. He demanded that I sing "The Star Spangled Banner," every verse, no mistakes. If I failed, even one word out of place, I would be required to pay him 25 cents, a not insignificant bit of change to a first-grader in 1963. "If you don't produce the money," said Gus, clenching and unclenching his fists, "then we'll just have to see."

A grim scenario, but it could have been worse. I didn't know any of the words to "This is My Country," and was shaky about the second half of "America the Beautiful" and "America (My Country 'Tis of Thee)." On the other hand, the National Anthem was ubiquitous in Cold War-era Arizona. We sang the song in class every week, a proud and assertive, if slightly off-key, endorsement of the idea of America. I had also heard it performed several times at the Arizona State football games I attended with my dad.

And I actually liked to sing. I had a high-pitched voice, not unpleasant to hear in my opinion, although it lacked the consistency and tone of a boy soprano. I had the musical tastes of a sentimental adult, preferring gorgeous melodies from Times Long Ago and Places Far Away, e.g., "Coming Through the Rye," "Greensleeves," "The First Noel." Not having an older sister or with-it parents, I was oblivious to pop and rock and roll. I'm not sure I had heard of Elvis Presley, let alone Chuck Berry, Little Richard, or Buddy Holly. I didn't discover the music of the 1950s until the 1970s.

Gus didn't set any preconditions regarding tune, or pitch, but I felt it was in my best interest to offer as faithful a rendition as possible. It would have been both humiliating and embarrassing to fail because I destroyed the melody.

The block remained deserted. We'd gone from classic western to sci-fi thriller, the presence of a grotesque creature from Outer Space keeping frightened earthlings confined to their homes. It was as if Gus knew the right time to strike. After all, it only takes the arrival of a hefty 10-year-old in the proverbial white hat to put an end to the malevolent plans of a chubby third-grader. But my potential rescuers had apparently taken the night off.

I closed my eyes and concentrated, like a concert performer in the final moments before the curtain rises. Gus regarded my "preparation" as a stall tactic, however, and in a tone equally impatient and downright rude demanded that I commence singing.

I made it through the first verse fine and the next one as well. But somewhere around "gave proof through the night" I messed up. I tried to cover my mistake by staying the course, as if nothing had gone wrong, but Gus wasn't fooled. It was just my luck to have a jingoistic bully who actually knew every word to the National Anthem.

My stumble delighted Gus. Wearing a wicked grin, he pointed out the obvious. I had two choices; pay up or accept my punishment, which at that point had not been explicitly defined, except that it apparently involved his fists against my body. One punch, two punches, shoulders, arms, legs, all to be determined.

But my bad luck was about to change. Earlier that day, my mother had taken her three kids to the local 7-11, conveniently located a short walk from our home. I was given a few quarters to buy candy bars, probably as a reward for having performed well on a test. I selected nickel and dime items and went to the checkout line alone, a self-reliant first-grader. I made my purchase and forgot to give the change to my mother. I promise that it was an innocent mistake.

By the time Gus blocked my path I had neither changed my pants nor returned the coins to their rightful owner. I would like to think my mother approved of what happened next. I stuck my hands inside my front pockets, secured a quarter, and presented the offering to Gus. Though I was paying off a bully, it felt like I had won some sort of victory, which was bolstered by Gus's evident disappointment.

My brute detractor had been denied the pleasure of demonstrating his ability to punch, without remorse, a jittery half-wimp. I posed no physical challenge to Gus; our so-called fight would have been over early in the first round. The question was whether he had the commitment to carry through with his threat. Could this menacing giant punch a defenseless kid whose only sin was to botch "The Star Spangled Banner"?

We will never know. Gus may have been a bully, but he didn't back out of deals, even those that he imposed through sheer intimidation. Gus grudgingly accepted the quarter and walked away, perhaps in search of another clueless boy to prey upon.

I waited a few days to share the details with my parents. After all, Gus had not committed an assault—there was no physical evidence that anything had happened—and now safe at home, the entire experience seemed to me more embarrassing than traumatic. I told my mom and dad the story without drama or pathos; just a straightforward account of a bigger kid who demanded I sing the National Anthem or else. Of course, they didn't like that their son had been bullied, but perhaps sensing my relatively sanguine state of mind, they listened without becoming too angry or recommending a course of action.

We moved to Southern California in the late summer of 1963. A year later, on a return visit to Tempe, I was walking down the street alone, in the middle of a sunny day, when I saw Gus with another kid, heading in my direction. What the hell was he going to demand from me this time?

I needn't have worried. "Tommy," he said, unaware that I was now just 'Tom,' "what are you doing here?" Gus sounded genuinely pleased to see me, like one long-lost friend greeting the other. I told him in a guarded tone that I was visiting the area for a few days with my family. Apparently absence even makes the hearts of bullies grow fonder. "What do you want to do?" asked Gus in a kind voice. "Football"? "War"?

I looked at his comrade, who had been silent the whole time. The kid was holding a plastic machine gun, his finger on the trigger. He and Gus had obviously been playing "army," my catchall term for pretend war. "Football," I said, decisively. The kid with the weapon protested, but when Gus brushed him off, the guy went home to sulk. Gus and I grabbed a football out of the garage and spent the next hour or so throwing, catching, and kicking.

Why the turnaround? Perhaps Gus felt guilty about having extorted the money. Perhaps he'd gotten bored threatening to beat up kids half his size. Perhaps the

National Anthem had lost its patriotic allure. I didn't question his motives. All I knew was that my former bully now wanted to be my friend. I suppose I could have told Gus, "Fuck off, you're not forgiven," which would have been rather heroic. But I wasn't that kind of kid. I was positively thrilled to be accepted into Club Gus.

This guy unwittingly played a key role in my interpretation of post-World War II American history. I have often cited him as evidence of the right-wing mindset prevalent in Arizona during the early 1960s, and the continuing link between bullying and chest-thumping, chest-bumping patriotism. He could have insisted on hearing my attempts at "Jailhouse Rock," "Blueberry Hill," "Runaway," or another selection from the pop charts. I would have surrendered without singing a note. Although those songs may have had a practical purpose, they mitigate the sense of terror that is critical to successful bullying. None of them is a call to arms, or an excuse to flex one's muscles. On the other hand, "The Star Spangled Banner" symbolizes the power and strength of the Greatest Nation in History. By failing to perform a perfect rendition, I had failed as an American, and had to face the consequences.

Despite the unpleasantness with Gus, as a young boy I didn't question the centrality of the National Anthem to American life. I fidgeted through numerous versions before sporting events, never wondering if it might be possible to end the irksome tradition without also undermining patriotism. I also presumed that my fellow citizens were united in their opinion of the value and meaning of the song.

That view did not survive 1968–1969, when I attended Willard Junior High School in Berkeley. The student body consisted of a nearly even split between Blacks and whites, and for the first time I was around a few colleagues who were dismissive of "The Star Spangled Banner." The majority of both races sang along, when required, but I also noticed Black students who kept their mouths closed. How, I wondered, could they get away with that? At the previous schools I attended, each of them nearly all-white, every student performed the National Anthem. In my case, patriotism was not the only motive; I was fairly certain that abstaining was against the rules and would lead to a punishment. In elementary school, I had an irrational fear of being punished. I actually cried once when I had to stay after class 30 minutes. I was sure the teacher would never let me out. The authorities had nothing to worry about from me.

But despite being raised in what passed for a mid-1960s version of a Progressive home, I also felt that I had a moral responsibility to participate. To consciously avoid singing the National Anthem would be tantamount to turning against America. I wasn't willing to go that far.

I was initially offended by the students who held back. Was "our" song not good enough for them? Was "our" country not good enough for them? I took their silence personally.

But after my brief period of resistance, I looked again, and arrived at a tentative understanding, for a litany of what should have been obvious reasons: slavery, discrimination, lynchings, the Klan, police brutality, poverty, racism. When one stepped back and considered the evidence, it made sense that a paean to America might seem hypocritical and profoundly offensive to a segment of the population that over hundreds of years had been often violently prevented from sharing in the nation's benefits.

In the summer of 1969, Jimi Hendrix performed a version of "The Star Spangled Banner" unlike any other, before or since. It was early in the morning, at Woodstock, and the 300,000 natives were sleepy, if not exactly restless. These huddled masses, already free, watched as a Black guitarist performed his vaunted electronic surgery on a song that had never seemed ripe for an acid rock cover. In the more than 50 years since that epic moment, among the most famous in rock history, no one can ever think of the National Anthem in quite the same way. Hendrix imposed his brilliance on American history, cutting through the thicket of tradition to a new understanding. Gus didn't stand a chance.

While we're on the subject, I never knew what happened to that kid who enforced his own loyalty test on a quiet street in suburban Arizona. Maybe he went in another direction, disillusioned by Vietnam, racial strife, Watergate, and other American traumas of the past 60 years. Or maybe he stayed loyal to the cause, voted for Reagan, George W. Bush, and Trump. Still, to me he will always be the patriotic bully.

CHAPTER 2

"Up With People"

Various, 1965–1967

In fourth grade I attended a mandatory all-school assembly featuring a miniconcert by the Sycamore Elementary School Glee Club, Claremont, California. For one number, the singers, who were in grades 4 through 6, performed a song I had never heard called "Up with People," which became the theme for legions of young people who toured nationally and internationally in the 1960s and early 1970s. The version that I heard featured loose and carefree choreography, including a moment when the performers pointed their fingers at the audience in a manner that they considered affirmative but to me came across as vaguely accusatory. They seemed to be saying that we had better take notice of and appreciate "people" — the common folk — if we had any intention of leading full and meaningful lives. I took it as an anxious plea to come together as a society at a time when things were starting to fall apart. Within a year, two at the most, the smiling, well-groomed proponents of this philosophy would seem hopelessly square, even to some youth who might have otherwise been their natural allies.

The simple optimism and comforting context of "Up with People" was both perfectly appropriate and comically inappropriate for Claremont, a city that was home to a world-renowned group of elite private colleges and was also one of the few in LA County with a Republican majority, a leafy, nearly all-white suburb that suffered more from the ill effects of urban, industrial pollution than did Los Angeles itself. A city that for all of its good liberal intentions was rife with nasty racism.

*   *   *

Living in Claremont for much of the 1960s made me ambivalent about summertime. Like any normal kid, I preferred no school to school, until my daily routine became its own kind of oppressive burden. I never went to camp, and the only time I enrolled in summer school, I dropped out after one week. From mid-June until the end of July, I would stay at home in the morning and watch game shows or play pickup baseball with friends, followed by lunch, either a sandwich, or hot dogs grilled on the stove, the only meal I knew how to make. In the afternoon, I would buy and trade baseball cards, and attend swim lessons. After dinner, I would listen to the great Vin Scully and the LA Dodgers on the radio. Off to bed between 10 and 11 p.m. and repeat the next day.

During the 1960s and early 1970s, Claremont was an ecological horror show in the summer. Throughout my youth and adolescence, I experienced a daily burning, grasping sensation across my upper chest, as if an army of stinging red ants was trying to escape. I felt the poison acutely during Little League practice and games, bike rides around town, or playing outside with friends.

Until my family moved to Claremont, I had never heard the word "smog." I had no precise term to describe the labored breathing, stinging eyes and smoke-filled throat that arrived every day around 4 p.m. Smog didn't only invade my body, it hovered above my city, a taunting, white film that civic boosters tried unsuccessfully to rename "haze." Our neighbors talked about the majestic beauty of mountains directly to the east of the city, but until mid-November of our first year, we had no empirical evidence.

As a young person, I firmly believed there was a reason for everything, a by-product of my interest in history, which started at age of 5 when I became fascinated by illustrations of ancient warfare. All phenomena could be traced to cause and effect; the Civil War, the Spanish American War ("Remember the Maine!"), the Korean War, and World War II. I even had an explanation for the outbreak of World War I, arguably the most complicated conflict in the history of the human race.

Yet, for several years, I was ignorant of the war being waged inside my lungs. I knew what caused the pain — smog — but what accounted for smog? The answer or answers were not to be found in any of the books or articles I was reading.

I was apparently not so different from mainstream society. In the mid-1960s the environmental movement had yet to become a cause célèbre of liberals and progressives, although it was Richard Nixon who started the Environmental Protection Agency. To residents of eastern

Los Angeles County, smog seemed both inevitable and all-powerful, eluding any attempts to impede its daily appearance and mocking the idea of California as the "Golden State." It sure wasn't like this when my family lived in Iowa or Arizona.

My environmental education began in high school, when I became a regular consumer of local television news, which routinely reported smog data. I learned such terms as "auto emissions," "sig alerts," and "parts per million," as well as the hidden meaning behind the euphemism "hazy skies." I now understood that my discomfort and physical pain was caused by a combination of industrial pollution and leaded gas fumes spewing from the hundreds of thousands of vehicles traversing Southern California freeways every day.

Still, I couldn't wait to get my driver's license and contribute to the problem. I was a typical Southern California male who wanted to wave to girls from the safety of the driver's seat and listen to rock music at a volume no parent would ever tolerate. The make or model of the vehicle didn't matter, only the feeling of independence, which was better than freedom. Like millions of drivers across Los Angeles County, I could justify my contribution to smog with a dismissive: "What's one car, anyway?"

At that time, the early 1970s, freeway traffic was bad but not horrendous, and public transportation had become a distant memory. Gas-guzzlers still made economic sense: The first OPEC boycott would not occur until the winter of 1973–1974. If you were a teenager who wanted to get around there was no accessible, comfortable, status-enhancing alternative to an automobile, preferably manufactured in Detroit. I took my driver's test in a 1967 Kelly Green

Chevrolet Caprice with a massive engine. The next day I happily chauffeured my little sister to her horse-riding lesson in that same car.

But while I was pursuing the selfish lifestyle of a carefree teenager from a well-to-do Southern California suburb, environmental organizations and public officials had been taking action to reduce the amounts of pollutants poisoning my lungs. I started to notice the difference around the same time I got excited about the prospect of driving solo. I would feel a sting in the summer, but not a burn. I took deep breaths in August and September without the usual coughing and hacking. I could go for a walk in the evening — after the temperature had dropped — and actually see the mountains.

I still don't pay much attention to environmental politics, even with the current and pending catastrophe of climate change. The environment means science; beginning in childhood I was never enamored of science, which seemed dense and slow compared with history and literature. In my entire life I have not read more than 10 science books, including alarmist best sellers.

Still, the successes of the burgeoning environmental movement in the late 1960s and early 1970s played a profound part in my political development. For the first time, I understood — truly understood — that government has the power and during enlightened periods the inclination to make things better. I could literally feel the evidence inside my renewed lungs.

Growing up, I had a remote sense of government's beneficence, having lived through the Great Society and been told repeatedly that the New Deal saved the American economy from certain ruin. But I became a true believer when my breathing improved, and in the summer I could actually tell and feel the difference between haze and smog. Since that time, I have had periods of disillusionment with Democrats and liberals, but I have never for a second wavered from my view that on the whole government does more good than harm.

*   *   *

In Arizona, my parents were members of the Congress of Racial Equality, or CORE, at a time when the Civil Rights Movement was integrated. At the dinner table, I learned about racists and racism, which I associated with burly cops, vicious dogs, cross burnings, screaming mobs, Alabama, Georgia, and Mississippi. In my evolving mind, racism was abhorrent, immoral, and shameful, yet also distant and removed — an American problem but really a southern problem. Our white people were better than their white people, the semiliterate crackers with crew cuts, clean t-shirts, and evil smiles. I abandoned that safe, smug assumption after a disturbing encounter in Claremont.

I must have been 9, and my brother 7. One Saturday morning, we rode our bikes into town to buy candy at a drugstore known for its wide array of choices. Eager to get at it, we had carelessly parked our two-wheelers close to the front entrance, limiting the access of customers. After we had purchased our candy bars and headed toward the door, we had the vague sense of being followed. As we approached our bikes, an older man, probably in his late 60s, began to harangue us. "Are you white boys or niggers?" he asked. Because only a fool would direct that question at two paleface kids, we ignored him. But this vulgar bigot was not really interested in our ancestry. As he helpfully explained, only "niggers" would park their bikes in a place where people — white people, to be exact — might trip over them.

Racists don't need empirical evidence to practice their craft. There wasn't a Black person in sight, yet this guy went on for several minutes as if he had stumbled into the March on Washington. I was shocked to hear "nigger" used with such abandon in my presence, a word I associated with that vast region below the Mason-Dixon Line.

Equally shocking, this ugly epithet came from a truly old man, to my young eyes. The senior citizens I knew well — maternal and paternal grandparents — were kindly and attendant, patiently talking to me about baseball and World War II, laughing at my juvenile attempts to be funny. We had lived near some odd old folks — my mother cautioned us kids about getting too close to a female neighbor who I later figured out was probably an alcoholic — but I could handle eccentricity.

I learned from my encounter with this despicable old man that people with thinning white hair, jowly features, creaky voices, and visible sunspots could also be real bastards. I am reminded of that fact whenever seniors vote down a desperately needed school bond or deliver rants about contemporary society, substituting half-truths and untruths for facts, bullying younger people who try to present a rosier vision.

Nine and horrified, I allowed the old racist to continue unchallenged as we hopped on our bikes and sped away. Twenty minutes later, when my brother and I reached home,

I instantly told my mother what had happened. I quoted his outburst verbatim and expressed the hope that the man would die, at this very moment, preferably in a violent manner. Being struck and killed by a bicycle would be wonderfully appropriate, I suggested. Though I leaned toward atheism, I nonetheless believed that a supposedly benevolent god wouldn't object if a racist perished from the earth. My conscience was clean.

While my mother was pleased that I had inculcated the right political values, she gently asked me to tone down the revenge fantasies, which she could see were not so much cathartic as a trigger for anger and frustration. A few years later, I heard that the silver-haired racist died from a heart attack, which made me very happy. Or maybe I imagined his demise.

In August 1965, the Watts riots offered proselytizing bigots the opportunity of a lifetime. Much of the white population was terrified, especially those living within a 50-mile radius of the burning, looting, and violence. A grade-school acquaintance of mine in Claremont later told me that his parents slept with a shotgun under their bed until the National Guard restored order. According to the logic of white privilege, the riots were the opening salvo in an all-out race war, with suburbs next on the list of targets.

We were not in Claremont, but Berkeley during the riots, 400 miles to the north. Even Caucasian paranoiacs were not overly concerned that hoodlums from Watts would soon be arriving in the Bay Area. Still, that didn't stop racists from publicly expressing their opinions, like the old man who stood in the middle of a Berkeley barbershop where I was getting my hair cut and told us all that Negroes were pulling whites from cars on the Harbor Freeway down in LA and savagely beating them. The events this guy described never happened; he was repeating one of many sensational rumors disseminated by irresponsible media. Still, he obviously got a thrill, relaying examples of Black lawlessness to his small, but captive, audience of worried whites. It was as if the guy had been waiting his entire life for the Long Hot Summer to ascend.

A few weeks later, my family returned from Berkeley to sweltering, smoggy, quiet Claremont. As our station wagon turned right on Eighth Street off of Indian Hill Boulevard, two blocks from our home, we suddenly noticed a large object of some kind protruding from the second story window. My shocked mother identified it first: A Confederate flag.

I had already learned from my father to hate all symbols of the Southern Cause. He insisted that I refer to the conflict of 1861–1865 as the Civil War, and not the War Between the States. He loudly disapproved of a television program called *The Rebel*, which starred Nick Adams as an ex-Confederate soldier transplanted to the Wild West. He and I once watched a college football game on television involving the University of Mississippi, and when students from that school waved a huge Confederate flag in celebration of a touchdown, my dad was enraged. He taught me to despise the Stars and Bars before he taught me to hate the bright orange and black symbol of the Nazis.

I still have no explanation why a Confederate flag was flying from the second story of our home, which was located across the street from an elementary school. We never discovered who committed this act of racial vandalism.

Maybe it represented a response to the Watts riots; nervous and scared whites finding comfort and strength in an icon of white supremacy.

But solving the crime and determining motive was not the immediate concern of my brother, father, and me. We had to remove the flag as quickly as possible. How many passersby had seen it in our absence, and either thought the worst about the people living in the house or saluted their fellow racists? We sprinted up the stairs, grabbed hold of the vile piece of cloth and set it down on the attic floor, in joyous defiance of official southern protocol. The three of us took the flag outside and dumped it in the trash, next to rotting fruit, discarded meat, and cat litter, an appropriate resting place until the garbage collectors removed it forever.

*   *   *

I have never been comfortable with full-blown eccentrics, the kind who won't listen to reason. I encountered two such people — both women — in idyllic Claremont, and I still recoil at the memory, more than four and five decades later.

The first was the middle-aged proprietor of the Sugar Bowl, a shrine to bad teeth, as the name implied. This lady would often be absent from the counter for several minutes while puzzled young customers, clutching Abba-Zaba bars, Milk Duds, hot-dog-shaped gum and the like waited to pay for their health-destroying snacks.

Had my friends and I been so inclined we would have had no trouble leaving the store undetected. During the three or four years I was a Sugar Bowl customer, I never saw another employee inside the store, an extreme example of keeping payroll low. Eventually the owner would emerge from the back, half-awake and shaking, to ring up the purchases, without saying a word. I later heard that she was a heroin addict, although that may have been a 60s-style suburban myth. I was still in elementary school when the Sugar Bowl closed. Although not a surprise, given the store's dysfunctional business model, I still felt a sense of loss. It was the only establishment in town dedicated to candy alone.

In high school, I had another encounter with a strange businesswoman. "Scary" is actually a more accurate description. On a lazy weekday afternoon, I entered a pharmacy located in Claremont's friendly downtown to make a simple purchase, doing my part for small business. But as soon as I passed through the front door I knew that I had made a mistake. The shelves were half empty and there were no customers or employees, as if the owners had quickly abandoned the site without saying good-bye, forgetting to unplug the neon "Open" sign on the front door.

I have no recollection of the particular item I wanted to purchase, though it must have been medical in nature, since I waited several minutes for help as I recall.

Eventually, a woman came out from behind the back curtain, and she was frightening to behold. She seemed to be in her early 60s, was dressed in a bathrobe and slippers, and had stringy, ratted hair. I've never been a fan of horror films, but I knew enough cinema history to compare her appearance with the lumbering corpses in *Night of the Living Dead*. I should have run, but as a decade earlier with Gus the Bully, I remained frozen in place, if this time, weirdly fascinated.

She didn't say a word and looked at me as if I was the insane one. From the perspective of 40+ years, I can't say I blame her. She was probably wondering what the hell I was doing in her consumer-unfriendly establishment. Didn't I get the message that she just wanted to be left alone? The two of us stared at each other silently, like confused animals from different species. The standoff lasted a couple of minutes until I set down my purchase, and hastily exited the store, never to return.

Compared with creepy suburbs depicted in popular culture, Claremont by my reckoning was rather tame. I never had the sense that there were thousands of juicy secrets buried beneath the expertly manicured lawns. Still, I didn't expect to encounter adults like these two women; not in my hometown, anyway. I was raised within blocks of institutions dedicated to enlightened discourse and rational thought. Sure, we had some rowdy students and philandering professors, but that came with the territory in the 1960s and 1970s. Yet, the presence of middle-aged, middle-class women obviously experiencing some kind of mental and physical breakdown seemed like an intrusion. These were the kinds of folks you would expect to encounter in creepy backwater places.

I felt offended rather than empathetic, as if these women had come to Claremont with the sole intention of harming the reputation of my sophisticated little town. I have since become more understanding and entertained the possibility that their condition may have in part been a product of the times. Perhaps their already fragile psyches were pushed into madness by what they directly and indirectly experienced as mid-century American women, with minimal opportunities and outlets.

CHAPTER 3

"Mary, Mary"

The Monkees, 1967

I purchased my first album, *More of the Monkees*, at the age of 10, in the spring of 1967. After school let out, I walked to a local record store in Claremont, and as I recall, put $5.99 plus tax on the counter, and brought the LP home, where I played it from beginning to end at least five times before going to bed, but not to sleep. The songs continued to rattle across my brain, none more so than "Mary, Mary," which featured a sliding rhythm guitar riff and Micky Dolenz's vocals, a teenage plea for an elusive girl's attention. For the first time in my life, I actually counted sheep — into the high three digits, no less — but even that time-tested cure failed to achieve the desired result. I finally fell asleep from youthful exhaustion around midnight.

I have heard of and met peers who claimed to have watched the Beatles performance on *The Ed Sullivan Show* in February 1964. These kids were six, maybe seven at the time, roughly my age. I suppose it was possible, especially if they had a big sister. But I was the oldest of three, and my parents, Nancy and Theodore Waldman, were born in 1924 and 1925, respectively. The Beatles' debut was a nonevent in our house.

What really turned me on was war and baseball.

*   *   *

I first learned about World War II on December 7, 1961, the 20th anniversary of the attack on Pearl Harbor. In kindergarten, I usually took the bus to school. On the day I was introduced to WWII, however, I received a ride to campus from my mother, always a treat because of the conversation and door-to-door service. Along the route, maybe two miles in total, I couldn't help but notice the sheer number of American flags on display, well above the patriotic norm; on front lawns, attached to porches, poised for takeoff from second-story house frames. I asked my mother; why all the red, white, and blue?

Sixteen years after the end of the war, the racist term "Japs" was still commonly used, though not by our family. She explained to me that on this date in 1941, Japanese planes bombed an American naval base in Hawaii called Pearl Harbor. The sneak attack killed thousands of U.S. sailors, many of them aboard the U.S.S. Arizona, which my mom figured was the reason for the excessive number of flags in our hometown of Tempe.

I would never again witness such a grandiose commemoration of Pearl Harbor Day. By the end of the 1960s — the height of the Vietnam War — the December 7th remembrances were comparatively modest. For me, it was an early lesson that how we acknowledge the past is itself subject to the whims of history. Some 30 years later, the second attack on America took away some of the luster of the first. Over the subsequent two decades, the events commemorating 9/11 have far exceeded recent official ceremonies marking the bombing of Pearl Harbor, even on the 75th anniversary in 2016.

In her high-speed summary, my mother didn't stop at December 7, 1941, but continued on with the story, as if it would not be proper to leave me in suspense about the outcome. Pearl Harbor led to America entering World War II. The U.S. fought the Germans and the Japanese, from 1941 to 1945, and prevailed, with the help of Britain and the Soviet Union. She might have singled out D-Day for special mention.

For a young boy, all history is military history. No root causes, no political blunders, no diplomatic overtures, no home front, no strong leaders, no industrial might. For me, history didn't exist beyond M1-rifles, machine guns, tanks, bombs, fierce fighting, and death, in the abstract. Even Hitler was a sideshow. In contrast to dreary numbers on a workbook page, or routine stories in some generic primer, history was thrilling, loud, and vivid, more present than past.

My family didn't have any books about WW II, or to be specific, books with pictures, but we did have a television. Under the care of a friendly teenaged babysitter who didn't especially concern herself with official bedtimes, I watched *The Desert Fox* on a Saturday night in 1962. The film featured the English actor James Mason playing the German general

Erwin Rommel. I would have preferred more battle scenes, but it was still exciting to see World War II on screen for the first time: Nazi generals in long black leather coats, soldiers in uniform, planes, tanks, jeeps, machine guns.

In the spring of 1963, the father of David Wise, my good friend and neighbor, took the two of us to the local drive-in to see a film called *Miracle of the White Stallions*, the real-life story of the rescue of the Lipizzaner Stallions from Vienna during the Second World War. David's family was Mormon, and they always seemed to be hosting church functions that involved Lemon Meringue pie. If there were leftovers, David's kindly mother would offer me a piece, without any ulterior motive. David mentioned Jesus from time to time, but not in an aggressive or pushy manner, and so far as I could tell never with the obvious intention of adding me to the Mormon population.

At one point during the *Miracle of the White Stallions*, I seized an opportunity to demonstrate just how much I had learned about World War II. The specific reason escapes me now, but I cut into the dialogue to note that the United States and the Soviet Union were allied against the Nazis. David immediately dissented. In the early 1960s, it didn't seem possible that the U.S. and U.S.S.R. could have ever been on the same side, especially to a young kid growing up amidst the anti-Communist hysteria of Arizona.

In fact, the Cuban Missile Crisis had occurred only a few months earlier. During one of those fateful 13 days in October, my first-grade teacher sent the students home with a note about what to do if a nuclear war began while we were in class. For the fifth- and sixth-graders — born in the early 1950s, familiar with fallout shelters and the like — the information must have seemed like old news, but not to me.

This typical public school note — grey-blue lettering on flimsy white paper, smelling of carbon — served as my introduction to the terrors of the atomic age.

*   *   *

In the summer of 1963, my family moved to Claremont, a college town 35 miles east of Los Angeles, where my dad accepted a position as professor of philosophy at Harvey Mudd College, the second relocation of my young life. I had been born in Iowa, and lived there until the summer of 1961, when my father took a teaching job at Arizona State University. I was pleased by the latest move, mostly because I now had local sports teams to root for. The California myth was about to explode — Beach Boys, beach movies, folk rock — but I was too young to appreciate its sensual benefits, let along partake in them.

I was in the Sycamore Elementary School cafeteria having lunch on November 22, 1963, when I learned about the assassination of President Kennedy. My first thought was that they were going to have to change the milk carton with a minibio of President John Fitzgerald Kennedy (JFK) to include the year of his death. When I went out to the playground, a sixth grader was re-enacting the shooting of the president, his arms extended as if holding a rifle. At that point, I didn't know any details of the crime, including how it was done or the name of the suspect. I got my information, piecemeal, from other kids.

Teacher training manuals do not offer guidelines on how to talk to your students in the event of a presidential assassination. At my school, the faculty improvised. I heard that some teachers cried, although I didn't personally witness any examples of that. My second-grade teacher, Mrs. Priscilla Ellithorpe, calmly discussed the president and his family, and even spoke about his political legacy, providing her own first draft of history. She noted that we had a kid in the class, Brian Fitzgerald, whose last name was the same as Kennedy's middle name. Brian seemed a little embarrassed by the unexpected attention.

In the early evening, I was driving with my dad in the car, just the two of us. On AM radio, there was continuous coverage of the events in Dallas. At one point, a woman who said she had warned the president not to travel to the city, was being interviewed on the air and over the phone. It was unclear to me if she had written a letter to that effect or tried to contact the White House. The story held a kind of masochistic allure for listeners, who were no doubt thinking to themselves, "if only, if only."

At that moment, my father asked, "Did you hear the president was assassinated?" He was making sure that this eldest child understood the historical importance of what had occurred earlier in the day. The last commander in chief to be killed in office was William McKinley, 62 years earlier, well before the birth of my dad. This was new to him as well.

I confirmed that I had heard about the assassination, from several different sources in fact. Before he could respond, I added an editorial comment: "You didn't like him anyway." A true statement — my liberal parents considered Kennedy a cold warrior — but not what my dad expected, sarcasm from his second-grade son in the wake of a national tragedy.

I was just old enough that my dad thought I might be serious. "I didn't want to see him assassinated," he said with a dry laugh, clarifying his position, in case there was any doubt. He also didn't want his son growing up to think that it was OK to murder politicians. I took his point, although there have been a few over the years that I wished would die in office. Don't be alarmed; it's only a harmless fantasy.

    *   *   *

By the time I discovered rock and roll, in September 1966, the Beatles had released 12 albums in America and who knows how many singles. At least two of the band members had dropped acid, and the group was starting work on *Sgt. Pepper*, which was an entire musical universe removed from "I Want to Hold Your Hand." I hadn't even heard of the Rolling Stones, the Byrds, or the Who. My knowledge of rock and roll was on par with an uninformed 75-year-old man.

I had missed it all, but I also didn't care. Between following professional sports, playing in recreation leagues, occasionally reading the newspaper, and watching war movies as well as the TV program, *Combat!* I had plenty of diversions.

My brother and I came upon the Monkees by accident. I was too busy following the Dodgers that summer — involved in another exciting pennant race — to note the hype leading to the first episode. The two of us were simply trying to find a program to watch on a school night before we had to go to bed.

I have had to occasionally apologize to friends that a group cynically assembled by Hollywood to cash in on the Beatles' incredible success started me on the path to becoming a lifelong rock and roll fan. It also hasn't helped that my introduction came via television, rather than KHJ, KFWB, or KRLA; vaunted AM radio stations in Southern California during the mid-1960s. But other than hearing Vin Scully broadcast the Dodgers — including Sandy Koufax's perfect game in September 1965 — I couldn't imagine why anyone would listen to the radio.

I succumbed to the entire Monkees' package; long hair, trendy clothes, youthful wit, gentle spirit of rebellion, plus many exceptional songs, which I still love hearing. My brother bought their first album, and I bought the second, helpfully titled *More of the Monkees*. For the first few months, it didn't occur to either of us to purchase albums or 45s by any other rock and roll performers. The Monkees more than covered our musical needs.

Mom and dad reacted to my new obsession with a mixture of bemusement and mild disappointment. Being rather with-it and aware folks, my parents must have realized that eventually their children would listen to rock and roll, and like what they heard. But they were not at all pleased that we jumped in because of the Monkees, who were wholly created by slick entertainment industry types. Though I was only 10, they hoped that I would have seen through the gimmick, not been so easily manipulated. Whenever my brother and I brought home the monthly magazine *Monkee Spectacular*, my dad wore a look of disgust.

Near the end of the Monkees' first season on NBC, the spring of 1967, my mom derived a certain sadistic pleasure from telling my brother and me that she had heard the group didn't play their own instruments on record. I emphatically denied the charge and accused her of spreading disinformation purely to persuade us to drop the group. She smiled, insisted the story was true, but didn't pursue the matter. If we wanted to continue to follow these frauds, that was our problem. A few years later, I learned my mother had been correct, up to a point. The Monkees had not played instruments on their first two albums, but they played virtually everything on their third, *Headquarters*, still my favorite. So, we were both right.

My brother and I started spending more money on pop music than baseball cards, a once-unthinkable shift in our financial priorities. We bought *16*, *Tiger Beat*, and *Flip* every month and listened for hours to KRLA, the leading AM rock and roll station in the Southern California market. The Monkees remained our favorite group, but we also liked other solo acts and bands; the Association, Donovan, the Lovin' Spoonful, the Turtles, the Who, the Supremes, the Temptations, and Smokey Robinson and the Miracles.

Unlike a kid who started listening to rock in, say, 1974, my brother and I were lucky. We were seduced by the Monkees and the Greatest Album of All Time.

CHAPTER 4

"A Little Help From My Friends"

The Beatles, 1967

In 1998, I interviewed Peter Tork of the Monkees for a book I was working on about the intersection of rock and politics from the 1950s to present day. I had seen Peter perform at a small space in Studio City and asked a mutual friend and adult Monkees fanatic to make an introduction.

I met Peter at a deli in Santa Monica. We discussed Vietnam, folk music, and how the Monkees television show fit into the emergent counterculture. For a few minutes, we also talked about the Beatles, because every serious conversation involving pop music in the 1960s eventually gets around to the Beatles.

Peter Tork had been a huge fan of Little Richard, Chuck Berry, Buddy Holly, and other seminal rock and roll stars of the 1950s. But in his middle teen years he grew disillusioned by the rise of Dick Clark and his Philadelphia-based dreamboats, Fabian, Frankie Avalon, and Bobby Rydell. He switched his guitar choice from electric to acoustic, and his musical preference from rock and roll to folk. In early 1964, the Beatles came to America, and Tork switched again, loyal to whatever sounded new, fresh, and innovative at the moment.

When I asked if there was one song that made the difference, he didn't name "I Want to Hold Your Hand," "All My Loving," or "That Boy," three of the numbers performed on the *Ed Sullivan Show*. Instead, he offered "She Loves You," which was one of a flurry of Beatles' 45s released in the early spring of 1964 on labels other than Capitol. Peter took a drag from his ever-present cigarette, looked me directly in the eye, and in a tone that blunted any dissent, declared "Music has still not caught up to 'She Loves You."

It was quite a compliment to pay to a song that had been released 35 years earlier, before Cream, the Grateful Dead, Pink Floyd, Yes, Genesis, and for that matter, *Sgt. Pepper*. But the more I thought about it, the more Tork's comment made sense.

"She Loves You" is presented in the form of constructive advice, peer to peer, which is almost unheard of in the "I, Me, Mine" world of pop lyrics. It opens with the chorus, also highly unusual, but a brilliant decision, as time has demonstrated. Today, "She loves you (yeah, yeah, yeah)" is one of the best-known Beatles' lines, along with "Yesterday" ("All my troubles seemed so far away") and "A Day in the Life" ("I read the news today, oh boy"). The stop-and-go ending is another genius touch. "She Loves You" is one of the few pop singles from the early 1960s that could easily continue beyond the three-minute mark.

And yet it took *me* several years to catch up to "She Loves You." When I started liking the Beatles, in the spring of 1967, they seemed amused if not embarrassed by their early material. On "All You Need is Love," Paul McCartney mocked "She Loves You," in particular "Yeah, Yeah, Yeah," as if he were inviting the rest of us to move on.

         *   *   *

I have almost nothing in common with Millennials, which is fine with me and I would suspect fine with them as well. Though I use social media — sparingly — I hate myself for doing so. I believe in gender fluidity but I couldn't name more than four distinct sexual identities. Other than "Shake It Up" and "Happy" I don't know any songs released in the 2010s.

Yet for all the differences, like a large number of Millennials, I was introduced to the Beatles through my parents, or in this case, parent. In June 1967, my father returned from a trip to Canada with copies of *Sgt. Pepper's Lonely Hearts Club Band* and *Bob Dylan's Greatest Hits, Volume 1*. I think the records were intended as a family present, rather than for me and my brother exclusively.

Either way, I wasn't going to fight my dad for the Dylan collection. As a mere 10-year-old, I was under no pressure to "like" or "appreciate" Dylan to prove my intellectual credentials. I preferred lyrics that were simple and easy to recall rather than obscure and profound, and I gave no bonus points for poetry. Because I didn't acknowledge, let alone understand love, romance, or sex, there was no point in trying to woo me with witty stories. Melody, harmony, rhythm, and a few basic rhymes were all that I required.

By contrast, even at 10, I was supposed to like the Beatles. The kids at Sycamore Elementary School liked the Beatles; even my 5th-grade teacher, Mr. Scoggin, liked the Beatles. He was a fierce ukulele player who wrote the lyrics to "Yellow Submarine" and "Yesterday" in black felt tip pen on two-foot long sheets of notebook paper, which were visible from the back of the classroom. He led us in several group renditions of "Yellow Submarine," which had only been released a few months earlier.

Still, I was a Monkees' fan, above all, and through fifth grade, the Beatles remained a distant second. It wasn't a fair comparison—to the Beatles. I listened to the Monkees constantly and rarely to the English guys. *Sgt. Pepper* was the first Beatle LP allowed into the house, and I didn't purchase it.

It would have been impolite me not to play the album, like ignoring a guest. In fact, I was tempted by the inclusion of the lyrics on the back cover, which I later learned had never been done before, by any artist. I lay down on my stomach, in the large living room of our Claremont home, purchased for $25,500 in December 1965, and followed the words of each song as it played. To me, it felt like keeping score of a baseball game, which was one of my favorite nerdish pastimes.

With *Sgt. Pepper* I could appreciate the words and the music simultaneously, and for the first time recognize how they influenced each other. I listened to the album regularly; though not, like the hippies, incessantly. After a few weeks, I had memorized most of the lyrics, and no longer needed the assistance of the album cover. Of more importance, by the middle of summer, the Beatles had tied the Monkees on my evolving list of favorite artists.

*   *   *

In the winter of 1965–1966, the end of a year in which
the Byrds released "Mr. Tambourine Man" and "Turn, Turn,
Turn," Dylan played an electric guitar in public, and the
Beatles came out with *Rubber Soul*, college students and even
some professors started to really like rock music. The
cultural shift was apparent in the Waldman house, where
my 41-year-old father and 41-year-old mother began to play
pop albums at dinner parties: Chad and Jeremy, Simon and
Garfunkel, the Mamas and Papas. At that time, the Monkees
were only a concept, and I was oblivious to all leisure
activities except Little League baseball and shooting
imaginary German soldiers with plastic carbines. My
parents might as well have been playing Bebop or Dixieland
over the home stereo system.

But a year later, the situation had changed, dramatically.
I had long since disappointed mom and dad by choosing the
Monkees and shunning the rest. They tried to get me to
acknowledge my error, abandon Davy, Mike, Micky, and
Peter for pop artists with talent and sophistication, but I
courageously resisted their scurrilous propaganda. Looking
back, I recognize these interfamily disputes as a preview of
the music wars that would be a regular feature of my social
life into my early 30s. In many of those later instances, I
played the role of my parents, embracing what I considered
to be highbrow standards and good taste.

My expanding interest in rock in the spring and summer
of 1967 coincided with its enthusiastic acceptance by young
and middle-aged intellectuals across America. I witnessed
firsthand how a form of popular entertainment that only

four or five years earlier had been considered common, vulgar, and talentless by campus elites was now not only tolerated but admired in our leading institutions. In the fall of 1968, to take one example, I accompanied my father to meet a student at UC Berkeley, where dad was in the middle of a two-year appointment teaching at the Experimental College. On the wall of the student's off-campus apartment were the four photos of the Beatles included with the *White Album*.

During this time, my dad served as de facto FM program director for my brother and me. He would learn about new groups and albums from his Berkeley students and immediately share the information with his sons. He introduced us to Blue Cheer, Country Joe and the Fish, Moby Grape, Jimi Hendrix, and *Led Zeppelin II*.

In the late 1960s, it became *de rigueur* to be both well-educated and possess an extensive collection of rock LPs. Philosophy majors and philosophy professors were writing about rock in new publications such as *Crawdaddy* and *Rolling Stone* that treated the genre more seriously than it had ever treated itself. It's undeniable that these commentators — citing on occasion Plato, Hegel or much more obscure thinkers — introduced an element of pretentiousness into the pleasure-seeking experience of listening to rock music. My well-educated friends and I would ridicule some of these efforts, quoting out loud especially egregious examples of pompous prose.

But I have also spent hundreds of dollars over four decades purchasing collections of serious rock criticism. Since high school, when I began to take the arts seriously, I have sought out the works of critics and reviewers. Well-written criticism is not only among the most sublime prose;

it taught me how to listen, to see, to experience. I own collections of play reviews by Max Beerbohm, Robert Brustein, Stanley Kaufmann, George Bernard Shaw, John Simon, Kenneth Tynan, and the *New York Times* (1920 to 1970). My modest library of film commentary includes Pauline Kael, Stanley Kaufmann, John Simon, and *The New York Times* (1930–1970). As for rock, my bookshelf features journalism by Nick Kent, Joel Selvin, and Robert Christgau, plus memoirs by Lisa Robinson and Robert Hilburn, whom I profiled for a Studio City online entertainment site in 2009.

In 1980, at the age of 23, I got my dream parttime job; reviewing plays for the *San Gabriel Valley Tribune*, a midsize newspaper based 20 miles east of Los Angeles. I simply called the paper one day in the early summer and asked to speak to the arts editor, who happened to be available. I told him I was a master's student in print journalism at USC, had a passionate interest in theater, and would be delighted to review local productions, if he needed someone for that purpose. As a matter of fact, he did, and would I like to drop by the paper the next day?

I was paid $25 per review, and always received two complimentary tickets from the theaters, which I realized was standard practice, but it still felt special. As a reviewer, I loved entering the lobby. I would be greeted by a friendly publicist — usually a woman — who would provide me with a press packet and tickets, sometimes actually leading my companion and me to our seats. I'm a fanatic about being on time in any situation; as a reviewer I would take extra precautions to make sure that I was at the theater no later than 7:45 p.m. for an 8 p.m. curtain.

Once an actor friend of mine named Dave was delayed getting to my house, which in turn should have made us late for the production of *South Pacific* I was slated to cover that night. Except that when we arrived at 8:15 p.m., the performance hadn't started. We sheepishly entered the theater, under cover of dimmed lights, and found our seats. Not a minute later, the orchestra started. Dave said the production was waiting for my arrival to commence. I disagreed, although more out of embarrassment than conviction. He was most certainly correct.

First time around, I was not an especially good reviewer. I allowed myself to fall under the sway of the critics I was assiduously reading, especially John Simon, who along with his obvious erudition had cultivated a reputation for being snide and mean. I was not as snide, and not as mean, partly due to personality and that I was covering Community Theater in midsized towns across the San Gabriel Valley rather than Broadway and Off Broadway. But I was snide enough, and worse, I felt I needed to adopt that persona to honor the profession and justify my role. I would write something unkind about the performance of a member or members of the cast as if I were meeting a quota. Along with unnecessarily wounding the pride of an actor who was either fulfilling or pursuing a dream, the need to be caustic and cruel affected the tone and tenor of my work. Instead of considering the entire production, seek the good in it, I would gravitate toward the negative, and in the process hope to find some redeeming elements. This was not a prescription for sharp, coherent content.

I spent some 18 months reviewing for the *Tribune*, when I left to take another job, on the editorial side of the same newspaper. I have a collection of clips somewhere from my first foray into theater reviewing, but I haven't looked at them in years. I am not enamored of the work, to put it kindly, and I'm not proud of my approach to the work.

Thirty years later, I got a second chance, with much better results. A friend of mine named Karen — who ran her own blog mainly focused on dining and entertainment — connected me to her friend, Nancy, who ran a blog that covered the thriving theater scene in North Hollywood. Because Nancy sent her team of reviewers to theaters that had purchased advertising on her site, writing even mildly negative reviews was not an option. I was expected to emphasize the good elements and mention the not-as-good only if they were so apparent as to be unavoidable, like the guest who wanders into a fancy party wearing two different-colored shoes. I exercised this option only on rare occasions.

To my pleasant surprise, I discovered that deliberately seeking out the positive aspects of a production significantly improved my writing. Freed from playing the part of the caustic critic, I avoided the clichés one invariably falls back on when panning a performance. Instead, I had to come up with original, expressive language to explain to readers why I admired a particular aspect of the production, and why they would as well. I also viewed those readers differently from the way I did during my earlier stint as a critic. They no longer existed merely to laugh at my mean-spirited putdowns but as people with unique thoughts and feelings whom I was trying to persuade. And unlike my first go-round, the 30 or so reviews I wrote between 2011 and 2015 for Nancy's blog I reread often. Other than the slight veneer of sarcasm that appears from time to time, you would be hard-pressed to find anything in common between Tom the Younger and Tom the Older. I certainly am.

*   *   *

A little more than a year after I started reviewing theater for Nancy's blog, she asked to me to add a column on rock music to my duties. I said yes immediately, despite the fact that she couldn't pay me, which was also the case with the theater reviews. Beginning four decades earlier, when I was an avid, teenage reader of *Rolling Stone* and *Creem*, I dreamed about writing rock criticism. For reasons of personal and professional inadequacy, combined with a general lassitude, I never pursued that dream, even with the campus newspaper. I wrote a couple of book reviews, and an article on ticket services that gouge concertgoers and sports fans, but nothing about rock.

Nancy placed no requirements on my copy, other than length, between 1000 and 1500 words. Her blog didn't receive any advertisement from record labels; she simply felt that a pop music column would be a welcome addition, and I was the right person — the only person in her stable — for the task. I had the freedom to write about whatever I wanted, which not even *Rolling Stone* contributors could claim. I chose rock from the 1950s to the early 1980s, the era that I knew best. I reviewed CD collections — from the Knack to Creedence among others — and books — a history of *Soul Train*, memoirs by Harold Bronson, cofounder of Rhino Records, and Steve Boone of the Lovin' Spoonful. I scanned sites featuring upcoming rock music CD and book releases, selected what intrigued me, and contacted an always-helpful publicist.

More than straight reviews, my pieces were mini-essays, in which at times I incorporated personal anecdotes and always provided historical perspective. I was creating my own modest additions to the thousands of articles and books written about rock since the 1960s.

When I was a kid under the age of 10, I had the usual boyish fantasies of someday playing major league baseball. By the age of 11, I came to the sad realization that the Dodgers or any other professional team would never use me. But at the same time, I was developing a serious-minded interest in rock that would pay off quite nicely in the years. And, like so much else in the 1960s popular culture, it started with *Sgt. Pepper's Lonely Hearts Club Band*.

CHAPTER 5

"This Guy's In Love With You"

Herb Alpert, 1968

It was not until my early 20s that I recognized the talents of Burt Bacharach and Hal David. To a rock and roll kid with no appreciation for pop craftsmanship, their songs sounded middle-aged, slick, and clever to the point of annoyance. The nadir for me was "Do You Know the Way to San Jose?" — a title so ridiculous that I figured it had to be either a put-on or a mistake.

However, there was one exception, although I didn't know for some time that it was a product of the Bacharach/David machine.

My parents were fans of Herb Alpert and the Tijuana Brass, and through repeated playing of *Whipped Cream and Other Delights* on the home stereo, I became one, too. The first time I heard "This Guy's In Love With You" on my favorite and only rock and roll radio station at the time, KFRC in San Francisco, I was stunned to learn that Herb Alpert was the vocalist. Like everyone else, I knew the man only from his trumpet playing. (He did perform a solo toward the end.)

I was entranced by the melody, and the lyrics were comparatively straightforward, though the sentiment was light years away from my personal experience. I didn't buy singles then—except for the Monkees — but if I had, I just might have purchased this one.

Yet, what I recall most about the song was its strange juxtaposition with world events. It came out in April 1968, between assassinations. A romantic ballad (which reached #1 in June) released during one of the most tumultuous stretches of weeks in American history, particularly when you factor in Vietnam. Even in the rebellious 1960s, the charts didn't always mirror what was happening in society: Quite the opposite, in this case.

*   *   *

On Friday, April 5, 1968, one day after the murder of Dr. Martin Luther King, Jr., my sixth-grade teacher, Mr. Moss, led the class on a hike deep into the Berkeley hills, where we were surrounded by pine trees and silence. We discussed King's legacy, and the future of the Civil Rights Movement. I told my fellow students that I was so enraged hearing the news on the radio that I clenched my fists and called the assassin a "bastard," in front of my mother, who didn't reprimand me. When Mr. Moss asked who would now emerge as the leader of the Southern Christian Leadership Conference, I knew the answer, having first heard the name a few hours earlier on the *Today Show*. "Ralph Abernathy," I said, smiling.

Exactly two months later, I woke up early on a Wednesday morning and went outside to retrieve the home-delivered edition of the *San Francisco Chronicle*, my daily routine. As usual, I intended to start with the sports section. The previous night, the Dodgers had played a home game, and I had gone to bed without knowing the final score. I removed the rubber band, unfolded the paper, and stopped at the banner headline: "Kennedy Shot in LA Hotel, Two Critical Head Wounds." The story was accompanied by what would become the iconic photo from the assassination of Robert F. Kennedy (RFK); the senator sprawled on the ground, staring at the camera through dying eyes. I forgot about baseball scores and spent the next several minutes reading the hasty, cobbled-together account of the shooting, which had occurred less than six hours earlier.

I ran upstairs to tell my parents the news. As it happened, they had gone to bed before Kennedy walked through the kitchen pantry of the Ambassador Hotel. My mom and dad had strongly supported Eugene McCarthy in the California Democratic Presidential Primary and were in no mood to hear his opponent claim victory. Like most of the country, if my parents had been asked, "Where were you when Robert Kennedy was assassinated?" they would have answered, "At home, asleep."

We turned on the television and saw Roger Mudd of CBS News broadcasting live in front of Good Samaritan Hospital near downtown Los Angeles. He reported that Rosie Grier, a defensive lineman with the Los Angeles Rams and friend of Kennedy's, who had been within a few feet of the senator when Sirhan Sirhan started firing, "didn't want to talk to anybody."

My brother and I left for school. We had just set foot on the John Muir campus when a kid yelled to my brother, "Hey Waldman, did you hear about Kennedy?" "Yes," we answered, in unison.

The RFK assassination was the first current event that I obsessed over. I memorized to the minute the time the senator was shot (12:17 a.m.) and the time he died (1:44 a.m.). I knew the names of the people wounded by the gunman, and their occupations and titles. When I got home from school the afternoon of June 5, I watched the continuous replay on television of the chaotic scenes in the Embassy Room of the Ambassador, as the word spread. No reporters, just the sounds of a woman screaming and crying, men shrieking "God no," and a calm voice asking, "Is there's a doctor in the house." I wished that I could have been in front of the TV when the news was initially reported.

My friends and I didn't use the commonly heard phrase "sick society" in 1968. We were too young to have a basis of comparison and too busy enjoying ourselves playing sports and listening to Top 40 Radio. Adults had a different perspective, including Mr. Moss. On the afternoon of June 5, 1968, a kid in my class named Robert started to talk and laugh in the middle of a lesson, as if he were with his buddies at a Saturday matinee. Instead of punishing the rule-breaker, the expected course of action, our teacher simply said; "Robert, if you think that when someone gets shot in America it's a holiday, we would have a holiday every day."

CHAPTER 6

"Expressway To Your Heart"

Soul Survivors, 1967

I was raised by parents who fervently believed in racial integration. As a consequence, they vehemently opposed Proposition 14, a measure on the November 1964 California ballot that essentially said white people had the legal right to prevent Black people from moving next door, or down the street. I had a friend whose own parents' vehicle sported a bumper sticker proclaiming, "Yes on 14." Because of what I had learned at home, I thought his mom and dad were racists, although I never said so out loud.

On election night, my parents were appalled that 14 passed in a landslide. The result dampened their joy that President Lyndon Baines Johnson defeated Barry Goldwater, also by a huge margin, in California and the nation. Doing the math, many of the same people in the Golden State who voted for LBJ — the most pro-Civil Rights president in American history — also voted for a proposition that enshrined housing discrimination. I sympathize with pollsters who try to determine with certainty the voting patterns of white people.

As the 60s moved along, the idea of integration was increasingly ridiculed by factions within the Black community. Their motives were not so much reverse racism — although there was an element of that — as a desire to seize control over the narrative. Young Black leaders, in opposition to the tactics and strategy of Dr. Martin Luther King, Jr., promoted the idea of Black People determining their own course, without the assistance of white allies. Starting in 1966, the Civil Rights Movement included leaders such as Stokely Carmichael, dedicated to Black Power, a phrase that a number of once-supportive whites considered both hurtful and threatening. Around this same time, the word "Black" displaced the word "Negro" in everyday conversation and the media. From my perspective — an 11-year-old white boy who was just trying to keep up — "Black" seemed cool and powerful, while "Negro" sounded old, tired, and insulting to both races. I made the switch immediately.

Still, I continued to quietly support integration, even if the idea had become a distant liberal fantasy by the end of the 60s. I anxiously looked for signs that whites and Blacks actually enjoyed being in each other's company. I watched sports teams during games and observed social occasions to see if, or how, Blacks and whites intermingled. Any visual evidence of casual integration made me feel good inside. I needed some kind of affirmation that we were not two separate nations, despite what the Kerner Commission had said. I didn't want to grow up under a system of unofficial Apartheid; the races permanently hunkered down in their separate corners. I knew that whites were historically responsible for segregation, but I was not concerned with finding fault or affixing blame.

In the fall of 1968, Berkeley, California, became one of the first school districts in the country to fully integrate its school system, with busing as the means to achieve that end. I attended Willard Junior High School, which was my district school, close enough that I didn't need to travel to campus by bus. Although it's only a guess, I would say that Willard's student body was around 50% Black, 40% white, and 10% Asian and Latino.

About two thirds of the way through the year, a band consisting of Willard students performed at an all-school assembly. The students were watching the equivalent of a junior high super group, although we didn't know it at the time. The piano player, Peter Jaffe, became a prominent classical music conductor in California and the saxophonist, David Murray, emerged as one of the leading jazz musicians of his generation. The band consisted of four Blacks and two whites; a racial mix close to the Bay Area's Sly and the Family Stone, one of the hottest soul acts in the world at the time. I couldn't help but make the comparison.

I liked the Willard group even before the music started. Seeing Blacks and whites on stage, together in one music-making unit, was a vivid realization of my integrationist fantasies. It was even better that these guys attended my junior high school.

I have retained two vivid memories of the performance. The first is a member of the group named Mickey, who was dressed in black tie and black patent leather shoes, doing "the James Brown." Mickey moved horizontally across the stage at Mach speed while Black girls screamed and called his name. The second is Peter Jaffe hunched over the piano playing the opening riff to "Expressway to Your Heart," a massive hit the year before by a white group from Philadelphia called the Soul Survivors. A few seconds later, the band came in behind him, and the audience caught the groove, many of them dancing in their seats.

The coolest school assembly I ever attended and the only one that after it was over made me feel really good about humanity. But Willard was a complex place that engendered a range of emotions during the tumultuous year I attended, 1968–1969.

*   *   *

Before enrolling at Willard, I had a combined total of no more than 20 Black students in all my previous classes, Tempe plus Claremont. At my new school I exceeded that number in Mrs. Grissom's 8 a.m. choir class alone.

A couple days into the fall semester, a Black girl was walking down the halls calling "honky," "honky," as if she was searching for a lost pet. Her tone was even, but insistent. Unusual behavior, but nobody paid her much attention. Maybe I was weird for thinking she was strange.

Later that day I described the incident to a white friend, who laughed at my ignorance. "Don't you know what 'honky' means?" he asked. I shook my head. "It's slang for a white person. Kind of like 'nigger' is for Blacks." "That couldn't possibly be true," I said. I had never read any article or book that referenced "honky" as a derogatory term for Caucasians. My friend needed to check his facts.

Over the next few days, I conducted further research, talked to other pale-faced kids, and finally had to admit I had been wrong. That's the problem with attending virtually all-white schools. You miss out on the latest racial insults.

I started listening for "honky" while walking the halls, sitting in class, and playing baseball and football on the field at lunch. I heard Black kids use it, now and then, but not nearly as much as I heard them call each other "nigger," which was another revelation. The vile word that was off-limits to me, almost from the time I could speak, was being tossed around without regard by the very people who were supposed to be most deeply offended by its use. A couple of months at Willard and my views about race had been thrown into confusion. I clearly needed to spend more time around Black People.

I tried to feel angry, hurt, offended by hearing the word "honky," especially when it was directed at me. For once, play the part of a person who is the target of a racial slur. But I couldn't pull it off, even among white friends. The same thing happened years later when girlfriends or friends who happened to be girls — sorry, women — labeled me a "male, sexist pig." Because I didn't think of myself as a member of the tribe of white people, or white men, group insults had no context or meaning. Call Tom Waldman "stupid" or "lazy," and I'm going to get upset. But "honky" will never hurt me.

*   *   *

Until entering seventh grade, I knew almost nothing about James Brown, not having a particular interest in soul music. By Christmas break, I could recite the words to "I Feel Good," "Papa's Got a Brand New Bag," and "It's A Man's Man's Man's World." On the Monday morning after James Brown performed a concert in Oakland, every Black kid in choir class had apparently been in attendance, and they were recalling the best moments.

My African-American classmates were not as enamored by what I would conveniently describe as white pop music. One day a kid named James brought to choir class the Beatles' album *Revolver*, which contained "She Said She Said," "Eleanor Rigby," "Here, There and Everywhere," and "Tomorrow Never Knows," among the greatest LP tracks of the 1960s from any group or solo artist. I loved *Revolver* and so did everyone I knew, including my parents and their friends. But to the Black students sitting by James, *Revolver* might as well have been the latest release by the Johnny Mann Singers.

"The Beatles," said a kid named Willie, a look of disgust on his face, "Why did you bring the Beatles?" Normally quite chatty, a severely chastened James could offer only a meek, mumbled defense. "They're good," he said, or words to that effect. Willie and the kids sitting around him looked at James as if he had lost his mind.

How could anybody my age so casually put down the Beatles? No one I knew talked that way about the greatest rock group of all time except conservative old white people who had never attended college. But it seemed that James had violated some sort of strict racial and cultural code and was being made to suffer the social consequences. Staying true meant rejecting rock — "white music." James never brought another Beatle album to class.

       *   *   *

I have never understood the calls for a "national conversation," except as a form of liberal condescension. In a free country, the notion that the government would direct a national dialogue strikes me as inconsistent if not antithetical. I'm also not convinced that it serves a useful purpose.

At Willard, I had plenty of natural discussion about race, without being instructed to do so by agenda-setting liberals. For example, I had a long talk with a kid named Michael Smith, who at one point noted with a straight face that "All white people look the same." I laughed at the irony, which eluded him.

I had a year-long friendship with a girl named Kathy, who got up one day in history class and said she was "tired of being treated like a damn animal." It was an indictment of white administrators and teachers, although I was never quite clear what they did to make Kathy angry. She and I remained pals regardless.

In that same class, an invited Black male student from UC Berkeley gave a minilecture in which he offered a revisionist assessment of Abraham Lincoln. Highlights: Lincoln was not a friend of Black people, but racist, and he didn't actually free the slaves. These claims were a prelude to a larger indictment of white racism in America. At one point, the invitee looked at our teacher and told the students that he, too, was a participant in this oppressive system. After the speaker had left, the teacher, who was Latino, quietly expressed his disagreement with the view of Lincoln and the overall thesis, which implied no difference between the Caucasian kids in the class and Lester Maddox or George Wallace.

Still, to this day, I feel fortunate to have been present for the Cal student's wrong-headed interpretation of Lincoln and extremist take on white people. Rather than my fragile, seventh-grade psyche suffering permanent damage, I was directly exposed for the first time to the absurd views propagated by some members of the New Left, which had an important influence on my political evolution. I have always considered myself a liberal, yet I reject outright the narrow worldview and intellectually protectionist policies propagated by various groups that occupy space within the much-heralded Big Tent. My experiences from elementary through high school (1974 graduate) helped me attain the critical-thinking skills needed to develop my own political philosophies. A great era for public education, before the walls closed in.

*   *   *

When I started at Willard in September 1968, one of the first things I noticed was that a number of Black students wore buttons that said, "Free Huey." The year before, attending nearly all-white John Muir ES at the base of the Berkeley hills, I was aware of the murder trial of Huey Newton, one of the founders of the Black Panther Party, but not its wider implications. None of the kids wore "Free Huey" buttons at John Muir, although the Panthers' national headquarters were located in Oakland, just a few miles to the east. Huey was not an icon in the Berkeley hills.

The white students of John Muir, and our parents, had by and large not transferred support of the Civil Rights Movement to support for Black Power. Even after the assassination of Dr. Martin Luther King, Jr., progressive white families still believed in the early and mid-60s model of marches and civil disobedience.

At Willard, freeing Huey was not just a cause, but The Cause, as if the entire quest for racial equality depended on the outcome of his trial. Even the War in Vietnam didn't get this level of campus-wide attention. Many of the Black male students on campus affected the look of Huey and the Panthers: tight black leather jackets or black leather coats, fastened with a thick black belt around the middle, and sunglasses with tiny, tinted windows. When making a point, they would move their glasses to the tips of their noses, and allow you to look into their eyes, but only for a moment before the shades went up.

Until junior high school, the only people I had seen wearing leather jackets were white: the early Beatles, Elvis, James Dean, and the Hell's Angels. Distant icons — except for the Angels — in rebel garb. But the Black students who walked the halls looked both cool and intimidating, an appearance to emulate. A few years before Black leaders had worn suits and ties. In seventh grade, I didn't care for suits and ties.

I did feel a persistent undercurrent of racial tension on campus, which could be exacerbated by a chilling look, a hostile comment, a threatening gesture, all of which led to extreme caution, adherence to rigid rules. I knew white guys who planned their bathroom visits to coincide – they hoped — with the absence of Black bullies. Certain hallways were to be avoided during certain times. I got careless now and then and had to surrender a few quarters, under perceived duress. I made it easy on my antagonists, handing over the money before they had even explained the consequences of noncompliance.

White kids attributed these types of incidents to race, exclusively. We never considered class a factor, even though most of us lived in or near the hills, in expansive and expensive homes, while the majority of Willard's Black students lived in dense neighborhoods in the heart of Berkeley. We needed a Marxist to explain to us that the situation was more complicated than it seemed. It would have been enlightening to realize that we weren't targeted solely because of the color of our skin, but also the content of our wallets.

In our arrogance, we also assumed that the bad guys acted that way only against the privileged white students of Willard, and after the school day ended they returned to their all-Black neighborhoods and behaved like perfect gentlemen. In fact, my friends and I had no idea about daily life in Berkeley's Black community. Other than participating in the occasional intercity baseball, basketball, or football games, few white kids that I knew spent much time in that part of the city. Away from school, our tormentors might have hassled smaller, younger Black boys for money. Or they might have been hassled themselves.

Still, the greatest threat from these one-sided encounters was not to our bodies but our minds. The progressive views of my white buddies and me were being challenged as never before. The intellectual crisis affecting Willard's white students represented a microcosm of the crisis affecting moderate whites around the country at that moment in history. Three years of riots, Black Power, and an uptick in anti-white rhetoric, predictably exaggerated by the media, had confused and embittered many once well-meaning, correct-thinking white people. The campaign team behind Richard Nixon, Republican candidate for President of the United States in 1968, took note of the unease. So did former Alabama governor George Wallace, running as a third-party candidate for president. The country was about to enter a new era of ugly racial politics, from which it has yet to emerge.

Having come from the comparative placidity of all-white schools, populated by the children of well-to-do, it was inevitable that my peers and I exaggerated the danger. Not once during the school year 1968–1969 were the police summoned to the Willard campus to put down a major disturbance, racial or otherwise.

Some friendships formed across racial lines. For boys, sports served as a matchmaker. Attending school in the Bay Area, I was desperate for classmates who didn't despise the teams from Los Angeles. I met two; Duane, who rooted for the Dodgers, and John Hill, a Lakers' fan. John and I suffered together when our favorite team lost in seven games to the Boston Celtics in the 1969 finals.

As I mentioned earlier, I knew very little about Soul Music when I arrived at Willard. With the exception of the Supremes, whose records were inescapable in the 60s, I had no familiarity with the Motown catalogue, and even less with Stax Records. I also didn't think of music as categorized or divided by race. I liked the Monkees because they were the Monkees, not because they were white. And I didn't consider the Monkees progenitors of a "white" sound, whatever that might mean. (I later discovered that "pop" was often used as a synonym for "white" in books and articles.)

At that time, Black radio stations almost exclusively programmed records by Black performers. Only the white groups or solo artists who could legitimately pass for Black, such as the Rascals, broke through the color barrier. So-called white radio was more generous toward Black artists, although a song needed to have strong crossover appeal to make it onto the playlist. At Willard, I was exposed to a new genre of music, which was the staple of radio stations I now listen to as well.

I became a fan of Marvin Gaye, Sly and the Family Stone, the Temptations, and more. I taught myself on piano the ridiculously easy opening riff to Gaye's version of "I Heard it Through the Grapevine," which I played in music class for a Black kid named Daryl, who was so impressed he called over two of his friends and asked me to do it again. By the middle of the school year, I had become an expert on the current soul charts; performers, song titles, lyrics. My lifelong passion for rhythm and blues, soul, and later, funk began that year.

*   *   *

On Friday, May 9, 1969, one of my teachers took our class to People's Park, a few blocks from the Willard campus. The area had received media attention, and she thought it was important that the class form its own opinion. We roamed among the 50 or so squatters, who were smoking, eating canned food, and guarding their sacred patch of brown and green turf. Some of them were amused by the visiting seventh-graders, some paid no attention, and a few were clearly perturbed to be treated as artifacts in a sociological field trip. I failed to grasp the beauty and freedom of this makeshift community, which included members who looked to be barely in their teens. Moving from one person to the next, I mainly saw desperation and squalor.

This was not just any patch of occupied territory, but land owned by the University of California, which viewed the settlers as trespassers. The possibility of yet another confrontation between street people and the Power Structure had proven irresistible to local media, which explained their interest. Still, it didn't seem likely to me that law enforcement would attempt to forcibly evict these mainly passive settlers. I anticipated a soft stalemate, until one side surrendered, away from the glare of publicity.

I obviously misunderstood the stakes involved. Six days later, the cops cleared the park, and UC Berkeley students attempted to take it back, on the command of the student body president. As the situation deteriorated, I was attending school a few blocks away, unaware of the soon-to-be-violent confrontation.

In the first period after lunch — art class — a curly-haired blonde girl named Eve suddenly exclaimed, "A car is burning." My classmates and I ran to the window in time to see a funnel cloud of thick, black smoke and bright orange flames. The teacher halted the lesson and joined us at the window. I found out later that that was no ordinary car, but a vehicle owned and operated by the Alameda County Sheriff's Department, which was already in a foul mood. The People's Park disturbance was about to turn into the People's Park riot.

Around 3 p.m., our history teacher had just started discussing some aspect of the American past, when a truant kid named Eddie, red-eyed and choking, opened the closed door from the outside and yelled: "There's pepper gas in the halls!" The class took Eddie's announcement as a signal to evacuate, even though that meant heading straight into the source of his misery. We arose from our seats, as one, and without waiting for formal instructions from the teacher, abandoned ship. The teacher grabbed his stuff and joined us.

We sprinted through the murky halls and into the sunshine, which we figured would lessen our chances of inhaling the gas. A hall monitor or teacher, I don't remember which, anxiously waved us toward the gymnasium, like she was directing traffic at the scene of an accident. When we made it inside, I witnessed hundreds of confused adults and kids, most of them showing no outward signs of having been exposed to the tear or pepper gas. In eight months at Willard, I had never seen the student body this united. A whites-only riot had brought us all closer together. The gym had become a kind of sanctuary, an extended village square, where students of all races shared information, circulated and knocked down rumors, and gossiped about matters that had nothing to do with the madness outside.

Eventually, the principal announced over the loudspeaker that we were dismissed. The school had apparently arranged for parents to pick up their children and for busses to transport students away from the riot zone. I availed myself of neither option, but decided instead to walk home alone, a mile or so through the streets of northeast Berkeley to our Parkside Avenue address. I always enjoyed this journey, past homes of sturdy stock and distinct character, foreign cars in the driveways, Jaguar XKEs, various kinds of Volkswagens, the classic 1960 model Porsche in silver or orange. These neighborhoods seemed unusually quiet in the early evening of May 15, 1969; perhaps I was comparing them with the frantic environment that I had just left behind.

When I reached our house, my mother asked calmly how I was feeling. She had heard about the People's Park disturbances, explaining it had dominated the news, which I didn't know. "Yes!," I exclaimed, racing into the family room to turn on the TV. I waited impatiently through the commercials, until the familiar logo appeared, *The CBS Evening News* with Walter Cronkite.

We were the lead story, footage of confrontations between demonstrators and deputies, clouds of tear gas, that burning cop car. The report ran "only" three minutes, which was a bit disappointing: I had hoped our local riot would consume the entire broadcast.

Still, it had taken almost 13 years, but I was finally an eyewitness to history, confirmed by Walter Cronkite. I felt sort of famous.

When my family returned to Claremont, a month later, I had a war story to tell. And wasn't that, after all, the point of moving to Berkeley? It would have been terribly disappointing to spend two years in one of the radical epicenters of the world and come back with nothing of interest to report. We might as well have relocated to San Luis Obispo, or another quiet college town. I had been shot at and missed, so to speak, although with pepper gas instead of bullets. Still, those minor details did not temper my sense of satisfaction. In my life, the phrase "There's Pepper Gas in the halls" ranked right there with the "The British Are Coming," and "Damn the Torpedoes, Full Speed Ahead."

CHAPTER 7

"Love Grows (Where My Rosemary Goes)"

Edison Lighthouse, 1970

When my family left Claremont for Berkeley in the late summer of 1967, the Monkees television show was about to go into its second season, the Beatles were the top act in the history of music, and I had never heard of a song called "Cold Sweat." By the time we returned, in the early summer of 1969, *The Monkees* television show had been cancelled and the group was falling apart, individual Beatles were losing interest in being The Beatles, and I knew a fair amount about James Brown, for a white youth from the suburbs.

Not even 13 yet, and my two favorite groups were either breaking up or on the verge of doing so. I was old enough to feel nostalgic pangs for the music of my "youth" yet also young enough to stay engaged. I substituted KHJ for KFRC, listening some days for hours at a time, the quintessential example of a kid who was sacrificing his intellectual capabilities to the pop charts. I made it my goal to learn the lyrics to every entrant on the KHJ weekly Boss 30.

One of the songs I loved most from this period was "Love Grows (Where My Rosemary Goes)" by a hastily assembled British group with the odd name of Edison Lighthouse. Powered by a great opening riff, which led into a charming melody—verses and bridge both — and a strong vocal, the song sounds like something the Beatles might have recorded during the late middle 1960s if they hadn't been under the influence of drugs and electronic experimentation—which was precisely the point. "Love Grows," along with "My Baby Loves Lovin'" (White Plains) and "Hitchin' a Ride" (Vanity Fare) were intended to keep before the public a certain version of the Beatle sound in the wake of the group's dissembling. At that point, early 1970, England had nothing on tap to replace the Beatles. The country was in danger of once again falling behind the dreaded Americans, which hadn't happened since February 1964. Adolescent listeners like me — too young and square to be seduced by extended jams — benefitted from this panicked response. I bought "Love Grows" and "My Baby Loves Lovin'." Intriguingly, it would be years before I realized that the lead singer on those two songs was the same person: Tony Burrows.

*   *   *

When I started eighth grade, in the fall of 1969, I quickly noticed that several boys I remembered with short hair now had long hair. In the intervening two years they had apparently defied their parents and joined the revolution. Although I had wandered Telegraph Avenue and visited People's Park, I still looked like a kid who would have been warmly greeted at a Youth for Nixon rally. My brother, who had black, curly hair, was the one who only occasionally visited the barber, to the consternation of our parents. I was the good son who never let his locks grow too long.

Still, I envied those among my former and now current classmates who looked like they had just returned from Woodstock. They seemed older, self-assured, and experienced in ways that I couldn't imagine. It was as if they had skipped adolescence and gone straight to Young Adult. On the other hand, I felt as if I was reliving the first day of kindergarten, over and over.

Though I was back in Claremont, I arrived at El Roble Intermediate School that September suffering from an acute case of social paralysis. In the first weeks of class, I desperately sought out vaguely familiar faces, made few attempts to meet new people. Claremont was not the problem; I had just spent two years in Berkeley after all. If anything, I should have been experiencing reverse culture shock.

In fact, the problem was bigger than Claremont, bigger than Berkeley, and it encompassed the whole of human history. Dr. Freud would have identified it after one session. Yet, I experienced the effects without understanding the cause.

This was the year I discovered that sexual awareness and sexual development — mental and physical — are not distributed equally. On middle and high school campuses across the world there is an uneasy mix of the pseudo-sophisticates, the possible participants, the late bloomers, the painfully shy, and the tormented, who may do harm to themselves or others. Compared with these nuanced and complex categories, LGBTQ is elementary math.

I fit uneasily between the late bloomers and the painfully shy, although I had periods of torment as well. In eighth grade, I had few passionate fantasies, daylight or nocturnal, and I was a couple of years away from discovering the easy accessibility of self-pleasure. Although I had gone through sex education, the late 1960s version, which was silent on many possible acts and combinations, I still didn't have a grasp of the basic concepts, including body fluids and states of arousal. If my school had been so insensitive as to give grades in sex ed, I would have received no higher than a B minus.

But even in my ignorance, I could see that there was something different from before in the way that boys and girls acted in each other's company. The flirting, physical affection (some unwanted), hurtful teasing, gossip, and speculation about private behavior, often without a shred of supporting evidence confused me. I left the racially charged environment of Willard Junior High School for the sexually charged environment of El Roble Intermediate School.

After several weeks of remaining in the shadows, I made the unlikely decision to join a group of hippies, which included a friend from before named Mike. When Mike had short hair, he and I followed the Dodgers closely, even attending a few games together. We also played on competing little league teams. Once I became accustomed to hippy Mike, I noticed that he hung out with guys with similarly hair length, and girls in long dresses with bright-colored patterns.

I had enough of self-imposed isolation, and I hated eating lunch alone every day. I approached Mike, avoided mentioning the Dodgers, and asked if I could just kind of hang around. He was agreeable, and shortly thereafter I met

Andy and Phil, the two other members of the male part of the group. I took Phil to be the leader, by his sheer force of personality. This was a few weeks before news broke of the Manson family, which changed forever the image of the hippie-in-charge.

My new friends deliberately remained above and outside the prevailing social scene, watching with amusement and noticeable condescension the interplay between the "straight" kids at a typical California suburban public junior high school. They had no desire to join the majority, and didn't feel in the least bit ostracized, qualities that I found admirable. They had managed to resist the magnetic power of youth conformity, American style. Of course, as hippies they had their own identity, which in some places, notably liberal college campuses, carried considerable cachet. But at El Roble, the counter-counterculture was clearly in the majority.

Mike and his fellow free spirits played by their own set of unspoken rules, which I would eventually have to follow to become a member in good standing. The first, and most obvious, was that I would need to forego regular or even semiregular visits to the barber shop. Fine, not a big deal, my dad was a college professor who spent the better part of every workday among long hairs, and my mother loved the Mamas and the Papas and enjoyed the more melodic Dylan tunes. By this point, my parents must have been wondering why I still looked like much the same as I did in 1965.

I would also need to accept that certain cultural and political points were nonnegotiable. Any hint of support for the American effort in Vietnam was forbidden, as was even faint praise for President Richard Nixon or Governor Ronald Reagan. Again, not a problem, my parents would have sent me to therapy or a re-education camp if I had exhibited those tendencies. As for culture (i.e., rock music), the Grateful Dead bored me, but I listened constantly to Cream, the Doors, and Jimi Hendrix. I also thought my new friends would find something cool and rebellious about a fledgling hippie who didn't like the Dead.

I was accepted; we ate lunch together, spent time during breaks. From the outside we appeared to be one happy bunch. But after a few weeks, I had become bored with the company. The problem wasn't them, but me. I couldn't let go, allow my liberated side to emerge, which was essential to achieving recognition as a card-carrying hippie. Even with long hair, I still walked down the halls like an uptight kid, arms stiffly at my side, eyes averting people headed in the opposite direction. I continued to wear short-sleeved shirts, tucked into blue Levi jeans, and tennis shoes with white socks. The only drug I took or wanted to take was aspirin, and never more than the recommended dosage.

I drifted away before they asked me to leave. By Halloween, 1969, I was once again the poor, sad loner, consuming my bag lunch at the end of the bench. But my pathetic circumstances would not last much longer. On a whim, I decided to try out for the eighth-grade basketball team. My social life was about to undergo a radical shift.

*   *   *

Every so often, I forget that I'm supposed to be a poor athlete and perform well above my own low expectations. I enter a zone that I never knew existed, which vanishes as quickly as it appears. I have played thousands of pickup basketball games since my early 20s, and my all-time record remains six baskets in a row, none of them uncontested layups. This is not a statistic I share on the court. The good players at any level match or exceed my personal best every couple of weeks.

I wish I could remember what I ate on that morning in the fall of '69, the state of my personal relations, how I felt about the future of the world. I'd recreate the conditions and repeat the stunning results.

During tryouts for the El Roble eighth grade basketball team, I played tight, focused defense, dribbled the ball the length of the court with speed and dexterity, and made enough shots to demonstrate I could put the ball in the basket with consistency. At one point, after I had shown some smooth ball-handling abilities, I sensed that off to the side of the court, the star of the team, a guy named Todd who had sway and influence, was saying positive things about me. From that moment, making the cut was a mere formality.

In a matter of a few weeks, I had traveled from one end of the social spectrum to the other. My hair was a bit short for my hippie friends but way too long for the basketball coach. I needed to immediately go to the barbershop and request the kind of haircut where the electric shaver travels up and down, back and forth, leaving piles of beautiful curly brown locks on the black and white linoleum floor. When the barber was finished, I would look like one of those kids who provided a glimmer of hope to old people worried that all was lost with this new generation.

At that point, I didn't have enough invested in my appearance to be overly concerned about the results. I cared only about conforming to the coach's tough standards. Having miraculously made the team, I didn't need to create any unnecessary problems for myself. If some folks mistook me for a young Republican, well then that was too bad for them. I could become an undercover liberal, which was an exciting prospect.

Climbing into the chair, being fitted with a smock, I distinctly recall asking for a "regular boy's haircut," which as the name implies is a simple, common style. But either I didn't clearly convey what I wanted, which seems highly unlikely, or the middle-aged barber deliberately misheard me, the more plausible explanation. He and his kind were not happy in the late 1960s and early 1970s. The trend toward long hair was bad for their business, and worse, nobody seemed to give a shit. I have never seen the data, but I would be willing to bet good money that from 1967 to 1980, middle-aged and older barbers voted overwhelmingly GOP, the party of regular haircuts.

When I rose from the chair, and checked the results, front and back, I was not shocked, stunned, or especially disappointed. I preferred wearing my hair long, but if I had to go short, I guess this was OK. I paid the grumpy guy, selected a red lollipop, and walked home. The family may have ribbed me a bit, especially my brother, whose hair remained at hippie length, but it was nothing that even my thin skin couldn't handle. After all, they had seen me with short hair only a few years earlier.

However, my El Roble peers had no such frame of reference. In math class the next morning, the other kids sent strange looks my way, as if I perhaps resembled this person named Tom Waldman, but could also be someone else. It never occurred to me that I should have warned them in advance that I was going to cut my hair.

I was getting noticed, finally, but for the wrong reason. Toward the end of class, a boy named Steve, a cutup, although not in a mean way, said in a loud voice, "Who is that kid over there?" He and several students laughed. I chuckled and wore the smile of The Seemingly Unaffected: slight upward curve of the lips and happy eyes, the perfect representation of a pleasant guy with the inner strength to laugh when the joke is on him. One wag admiring the wit of another.

My transition from hippie to jock hadn't started well. I was already somewhat suspect with my teammates, who were wary of my liberal politics, college professor father, and Berkeley connection. As far as I could tell, the white members of the team (only two players were Black) came from strongly conservative, typically suburban families. These guys wore their hair short before the season started.

One of them, a smart ass named Jim, stared at the New Me and had a revelation: "He's an egghead!" Jim didn't mean like Adlai Stevenson and his crowd, but literally, as in my newly shorn head resembled the shape of an egg. Jim was white — blond, loud, charismatic, and he had a pretty good shot, if a little flat upon release. He was not the team leader, but sufficiently high up the chain that the others occasionally followed him. This was one of those times. Within a few days, he had most of the guys calling me "egghead," which was subsequently shortened to just "Egg." Throughout the entire season, early November through early April, I would estimate that the ratio of "Egg" to "Tom" was around 20 to 1. Some of the guys even forgot my actual name.

My appearance and manners did not go unnoticed by my teammates, most of whom lived in northern Claremont, the conservative part of town. On a few occasions, I was told to "wash my face," followed by laughter. It was possible that I had missed a few spots, but was pointing it out all that funny? Another time, watching a game from the bench, my usual viewing spot, I happened to be sitting with my pale, white legs crossed at the knee, right elbow on right thigh, finger and knuckles over my lips. "Egg, quit sitting like a girl," commanded Craig, a backup forward.

His remark garnered the predictable snickers. I hadn't yet learned that "sitting like a girl" violated the male code, or even that there was a male code. At that time, I was so ignorant of girls and their natural habits that I didn't know what I didn't know, about sitting, peeing, periods, or bras. Still, I uncrossed my legs — I didn't need another round of teasing from the guys — and proceeded to slump and sprawl across the bench, in imitation of a real man.

Craig and I teased each other constantly, made snide comments back and forth, picked on each other's clothes, appearance, and politics. In the manner of films set in English boarding schools — without the furtive sex — we both sought the favor of a third boy, Andy. Andy had been Craig's good friend, but he was much too nice for Craig, and he had the good taste to enjoy my company as well. He remained close to Craig, while also making time for me, even spending the night once or twice. Craig didn't express any obvious signs of anger, disappointment, or jealousy about Andy's moves in my direction, but his actions indicated that he was none too pleased about my claims on his friend's time.

One night at practice Craig and I engaged in nonstop sniping, covering a multitude of subjects. We exhibited no self-control, and kept at it well beyond acceptable limits, even for a group of eighth-grade boys. The other players were alternately amused and distracted by our marathon of whine. Finally, the coach, a man named Jack, who was the quintessential human bulldog — flat, hairless head, neck shaped like a thick stump, the bark of a drill sergeant—blew a loud whistle, halting the drills. In the now quiet gym, he walked over to Craig and me and offered a few predictable comments about our immaturity and lack of awareness.

The coach then meted out a punishment that was anything but predictable. He ordered the two of us to clasp hands and take a couple of laps around the court. The other players, now voyeurs, giggled as they prepared to watch the show. Some of them may have been embarrassed, some of them may have been appalled, and some of them may have been quietly fascinated. But group laughter enabled our teammates to respond as one, disguise any confused feelings. At that age, most guys instinctively recoil from any affectionate physical contact with members of the same sex. I had never held hands with a girl before, and now I was being commanded to do so with a boy. Not just any boy, but one I couldn't stand.

I had never openly challenged an authority figure, and wasn't about to start now, even though Coach Jack had a weird way of disciplining Craig and me. I took the pragmatic view that refusing to go along would only make things worse. Craig didn't protest either. We looked at each other, red-faced but resigned, guilty as charged.

Craig and I clasped our hands by the fingertips and jogged around the court, trying not to fall while remaining linked. We didn't look at each other, but dutifully smiled for our fans, who responded with a steady chorus of cackles and chuckling. The two of us carried out our responsibilities brilliantly. With no time for analysis or preparation, we did a masterful job improvising our roles. Had this been an American version of the typical English boarding school film, we would have gotten the parts.

Although it seemed far longer, our handheld jog lasted no more than five minutes. After it was over, Craig and I rejoined the team for the rest of the practice. We didn't fuss or fight; just layup lines, rebounding drills, the weave, and free throws. Who knew what punishment Jack would devise if we misbehaved again? The other players acted as if nothing unusual had happened. For the rest of the year, the incident rarely came up.

When I got home that night, I neglected to tell my parents about the punishment, not out of embarrassment or shame, but because there didn't seem to be a compelling reason. Although in my life it was not common to see boys or men holding hands, I didn't consider such displays of male affection outside the realm of possibility. I would have been more embarrassed to recount details of the silly, relentless teasing that triggered the event.

Had this happened in the 2000s or 2010s, however, it would not have remained an internal matter only. There are too many cell phones and too many tempting opportunities to exploit the cultural, political, and sociological ramifications of two members of the eighth-grade boys' basketball being punished in this odd fashion.

Fox News, for one, would have found the story impossible to turn down. You can imagine the guest list; a religious leader decrying the ever-expanding homosexual agenda; a Fox-friendly therapist talking about the possibility of sexual confusion, even psychological damage; the principal of the school, who is implored on TV to terminate the coach immediately; and, if Fox is lucky, the coach himself, grilled by a hostile and incredulous interviewer.

Oh, and the coup de grâce, Craig and I appearing as guests, accompanied by our parents, the entire group instructed by the producer to appear properly distraught. Other media outlets would have followed, not all of them adopting Fox's strident antihomosexual line. Liberal stations would have decried the homophobic commentary while acknowledging that the punishment was a bit strange. For a solid week, two eighth-grade boys from Claremont, CA, would have turned into the most famous hand-holding adolescents in America.

I'm attracted to fame and have even enjoyed it in limited measures. But I feel only a sense of relief that this incident attracted no notice beyond the little group of spectators who watched it unfold in real time. I wouldn't want to be a national spokesperson or symbol because of some off-the-wall punishment meted out during an eighth-grade basketball practice.

CHAPTER 8

"Metal Guru"

T. Rex, 1972

By the summer of 1971, I started to drastically reduce my daily intake of pop music. I had become bored by the songs on AM radio, and I didn't have the patience to listen to extended album cuts on FM radio. I would tune in now and then, but nothing like the concentrated effort of the previous two years. Top 10 hits came and went without my knowing the artists, melodies, titles, or lyrics. In my heyday, I would sing entire verses from songs that barely cracked the Top 40. At 14, however, I was fast becoming an ex-rock fan. And I didn't care.

Living in London revived my interest. From February 1972, when my family arrived there on a six-month sabbatical, through early August, when we returned to California, my brother, sister, and I spent nearly every Thursday evening watching *Top of the Pops* on the BBC. In its format, *Top of the Pops* was similar to television programs in the United States—including *American Bandstand* — that provided a visual, weekly rundown of songs that were either high on the charts or headed that direction. But the British program had a charming irreverence that Dick Clark would have never tolerated.

For example, when the Move performed its hit "California Man," the drummer threw stuff at the audience rather than even maintaining the illusion of a guy keeping the beat. The regular dancers, Pan's People, performed choreographed routines that in some cases barely rose to the level of a talented American high school drill team. To a viewer — me — who enjoyed these programs but saw no need to take them seriously, the *Top of the Pops* approach was better than *Bandstand* and its self-important imitators.

I happened to arrive in London at a fortuitous time in the history of 1970s rock and roll: the beginnings of Glitter. America had nothing to compare, except perhaps Alice Cooper, but he was an outlier, not a movement. Glitter both amused and at times shocked my 15.5-year-old self, a kid who couldn't imagine going on a chaperoned date, let alone all the other stuff, starting with a friendly peck on the cheek. Every week on *Top of the Pops* I watched male performers in hot pants, eye shadow, and wearing outrageous colors play hard rock and roll. The first time I saw film of David Bowie he not only had the Ziggy look and hair but he was performing "Star Man" with his arm draped seductively around guitarist Mick Ronson's shoulder. This was a couple of weeks after a guy in his 20s winked his eye and pouted his lips at me on a suburban street in north London. I was not in Claremont anymore.

But the ultimate Glitter experience was seeing T. Rex perform its #1 smash "Metal Guru." The opening chords of the song featured a series of sonic explosions set to a simple drum beat with enough force and power to shake the foundation of Westminster Abbey, followed by the kinds of screams normally unleashed in bad horror movies. The studio audience leapt out of their seats, ran to the makeshift stage, and started free-spirited dancing, like hippies in Golden Gate Park. Surrounded by chaos, the lead singer peered at the camera through a thick mane of black curls, both oblivious and focused. After the opening shriek of "ya, ya, ya," his vocals turned sultry, which blended surprising well with the massive sound behind him.

The song was brief, maybe 2.5 minutes, like singles from the mid-60s, while the chord progression and saxophone accompaniment suggested the 1950s. Yet, the band members' brightly colored outfits and abundant glitter perfectly represented London in that moment.

I was too young to experience Beatlemania, but the *Top of the Pops* appearance by T. Rex couldn't help but suggest a comparison. How had I missed this group? How had much of America missed this group? ("Metal Guru," which was #1 in Britain, failed to make the charts in the United States). Were English teenagers that different from their American peers?

Before our family's trip to London, I had presumed that the Special Relationship extended to pop music. We liked their performers, and they liked our performers; the history of rock and roll in miniature. Wasn't that why John Lennon went crazy for Elvis, and Keith Richards spent hours every day trying to play guitar like Chuck Berry? On the other side of the Atlantic, wasn't that why we affectionately called it the British Invasion?

Yet, Slade, T. Rex, and a host of lesser acts I saw on *Top of the Pops* acquired only cult followings in America. I left behind the country where I had abandoned rock, didn't know, or care that the Raiders had a #1 hit with "Indian Reservation," or the title of Neil Young's latest album. I was willing to shed any last, vestige of cool in exchange for no longer being a slave to Top 40.

But in England I was being exposed to groups unknown to the vast majority of Claremont High School students. Although my former classmates were listening to the same tired stuff, I was on another level, the right guy at the right time, a swinging American virgin in still Swinging London.

*   *   *

In his memoir *Apathy for the Devil*, the English rock critic Nick Kent wrote: "These days, when people talk about the end of the 60s they like to say the decade didn't actually die until 1974 or even 1976. They're wrong: the 70s came into full effect in January of 1972 when David Bowie reinvented himself as Ziggy Stardust." (Da Capo Press, p. 59) Other rock critics and historians of contemporary Britain, have assigned particular significance to 1972, for reasons of culture and politics. My dad had never heard of David Bowie when he made the decision to move the family from Claremont to London between February and August of that same year. I guess we just got lucky.

On February 21, 1972, President Nixon landed in Peking, the start of his famous trip to China. A week earlier, my brother and I began classes at Haverstock, an English private school located in the Chalk Farm section of London, one tube stop south of our home in Belsize Park. Nixon may have had more in common with his foreign hosts than we did with ours.

My favorite teacher was Mr. Dudley, who taught religious studies. Dudley was short, wore horn-rimmed glasses, and had a mischievous grin and impish manner. He reminded me of the character of the Penguin as interpreted by Burgess Meredith on the *Batman* television show. When I first entered the class, and presented my papers to Dudley, he looked them over and said, loudly, for the other students to hear "Oh, you're from the Colonies." Out of respect, I didn't point out to him that I had never set foot in the original 13.

The rest of the class didn't seem to care one way or the other about my background. Being the new guy, I received the usual glares and stares, but none of the students made audible reference to my Yankee roots.

As a public school student in America, I had never taken religious studies, or even heard many references to organized religion in other classes. I grew up in a nonreligious household, the son of a father who revered that heretic Spinoza and taught Marx. My father was also well-versed in the Old Testament and recognized its literary brilliance and essential importance in the development of humankind and civilization. He had no problem whatsoever with my taking religious studies; in fact, he welcomed it. To be sure, the class covered the Old and the New Testament, but that, too, was not a concern at home.

I emerged from religious studies with my beliefs intact, and my knowledge of the world enhanced. I even received an "A" from Dudley, who generously put aside any preconceived notions he may have had about the intellectual capabilities of students who hailed from across the Atlantic.

In America, the term "Bible Study" has for progressives become synonymous with evangelical Christians — including Republican members of Congress — sitting in a room, bowing their heads and praying, interpreting the world in a way that is at best inconsistent with liberal values, and at worst, a clear and present danger to them. I would feel about as comfortable in such a setting as I would at the annual convention of the National Rifle Association. But the Bible study I experienced in London was quite different, and not at all disconcerting; acquisition of knowledge, no attempts to proselytize. I would recommend the class to any secular, teenaged Americans lucky enough to be in England for part or all of high school.

*   *   *

In my breezy preparation for living in England, I neglected to do research into the peculiarities of the Cockney accent. I was vaguely aware that not everyone in the country spoke like Sir John Gielgud when he would appear on *The Dick Cavett Show*, but I also had no idea how difficult it would be to understand the sentences uttered by many of my classmates, or people on the streets. When that accent is filtered through a kid born in Cyprus, you have the potential for a nearly insurmountable language barrier.

His name was Nick, and one of the questions he asked that I did instantly comprehend was whether it was true that Miami Beach was entirely made of marble. I had never been to Miami and knew the city only from watching the Orange Bowl and reruns of *The Jackie Gleason Show*, but I nevertheless felt confident to respond in the negative.

Another time Nick chided me that the best rock and roll bands came from England, not the United States. I had to concede the point, but I also reminded him about the Beach Boys and Creedence Clearwater Revival, both based in my home state.

But when Nick posed a particular question before school one morning the two of us experienced a full-scale communication breakdown. The fact that one of the key words began with an "H" was at the root of our difficulties. For reasons that I have never understood, the Cockney alphabet has 25 letters, with a gap between "G" and "I".

In this case, Nick asked me "Did you get your 'air cut?" To which I responded, "What?" He tried again, "Did you get your 'air cut?" To which I responded, again, "What?" These nonproductive exchanges continued for another couple of minutes, until Nick helpfully pointed to his own lengthy locks, and I finally got his meaning. For the entire time we lived in London, I never grasped the subtleties of the Cockney accent.

*   *   *

Arriving in London, I had attended no rock concerts, a couple of plays, both amateur productions, very few museums, and watched the vast majority of my films at the local Claremont cinema or nearby drive-in theaters. But after six months, I was a certified patron of the arts, in my own fertile mind.

My education actually began in Edinburgh in April, at a Scottish National Theater production of Ibsen's *The Master Builder*, which was playing a few blocks from the hotel where my family was staying. I had been invited by my parents, who thought it would be a good idea to expose me to serious theater. At that point, my play going experience consisted of watching a few scenes from a Claremont High School performance of *Bye Bye Birdie,* a production of Gilbert and Sullivan's *Mikado* at Pomona College in 1967, and my own starring role as Jack in the 1968 production of *Puss and Boots* at John Muir Elementary School in Berkeley.

The role of Solness in *The Master Builder* was played by an actor named Andrew Cruickshank, who looked like my maternal grandfather, wide girth and thinning white hair, neatly parted. Cruickshank made several speeches in a rich baritone that to my admittedly untrained ear sounded like the quintessence of British stagecraft. The female lead was played by an actress whose name I don't recall, although I recall well her performance. In most scenes, she wore a white blouse, a light-colored skirt, and a white boater on her head. I could clearly see her wide, shimmering eyes, even from the balcony. The actress circled Cruickshank in long, threatening strides, like an aggressive bird lining up its prey.

At the curtain call, I withheld my applause, profoundly disappointed to be reminded by theater courtesy that the characters had been played by real people, whose performances we were now expected to acknowledge. I had become so engrossed in the story that I didn't want my emotions to be disturbed; I filed quietly out of the theater, as the audience does after seeing a powerful film. When I complained to my father, he politely allowed that I had an interesting point, but he also noted that the tradition of applauding the cast was probably not going to fade anytime soon. If I wanted to continue attending plays, I would just have to accept that. Reluctantly, I pledged to do better next time.

A few weeks later, I accompanied Steve — a college student friend of the family who was also living in London — to a performance of Tom Stoppard's *Jumpers*. The house was filled beyond the rafters; the only time I've ever had standing-room-only tickets for a theatrical production. Of all the beguiling elements of *Jumpers*, witty dialogue, loony characters, piss-take on academia, I recall nothing so vividly as the moment the actress Diana Rigg walked to the right front of the stage and disrobed, for all to see. Have I mentioned that I was 15½ at the time?

At the time Miss Rigg came along, I had started to become acquainted with the pleasures of self-stimulation. Yet, I insist that my excitement at viewing her nude body was not purely sexual. It felt like I had taken another important step into adulthood, early 1970s variety.

Starting in junior high school, I developed a strong interest in the movies, and would peruse the entertainment section with the intense concentration that I would bring to the sports section, poring over data about directors, actors, plots, and ratings. At the time, 1969–1971, X-rated films were not nearly as common as G, PG, or R, but they were being released at a rate of one every couple of weeks: *I Am Curious, Yellow*; *The Damned*; *Futz*; *Midnight Cowboy*; *Medium Cool*; *Beyond the Valley of the Dolls*; and *Fritz the Cat*. A collector of trivia, I memorized the titles, even though I had no desire to see the films. The X-rating scared me off, like the "Keep Out" sign at a dangerous construction site. I imagined there was something dark and sinister contained within these films, which would result in terrifying nightmares, and a permanently damaged psyche. I gave my mom and dad various problems during my early teen years, but never once did I attempt to sneak into an X-rated movie.

My memory is fuzzy, but I believe Diana Rigg's character was having an affair when her brilliant and excessively neurotic husband arrived home unexpectedly — a plot device common to stage comedies for hundreds of years, except this time with a 1970s twist. The actress opened the sheet covering her naked body and beckoned her onstage lover to hide in there with her. She then carried on as if nothing were amiss — English to the core.

The audience probably saw Rigg sans clothes for 20 seconds, but in my recollection she might as well have performed the entire play in the nude. Ever since, I've told people with a wry smile that, as a teenager, seeing all of Diana Rigg in *Jumpers* is what got me interested in the theater. I even hinted at that in the theatrical biography I wrote for the program from my musical, *Eastside Heartbeats*, in 2016.

A few weeks later, my brother and I, along with our adult Welsh neighbor and one of her friends, attended a play about Aztec civilization in which, would you believe it, the same thing happened. An actress wearing nothing but a headdress briefly displayed her naked body for reasons that I cannot recall. At that point, nearly half of the plays I had seen in my short life included women in their birthday suits. What did I tell you about London in 1972?

*   *   *

At the beginning of 10th grade, I had started a growth spurt, which within a few months propelled me from being one of the shortest kids in my class to one of the tallest. In England, I felt even taller. Whatever their many virtues, the white English are not an especially tall race. I wasn't a giant over there, but I looked down on most of my classmates, in a manner of speaking. Had the English kids I knew at Haverstock School played basketball, I'm sure I would have been chosen first in pickup games.

My height proved to be an invaluable asset gaining entry to X-rated films, which in England like America were restricted to people 18 and over. As I've mentioned, the thought of attending an X-rated film made me queasy, all that graphic sex and violence. Until, that is, Stanley Kubrick's *A Clockwork Orange* was released with an X-rating. I had just started to take film seriously, reading the lengthy pieces by Pauline Kael in *The New Yorker*, which my parents had subscribed to for years. Subsequent reviews, far more positive than Pauline Kael's, and various feature stories about Kubrick, Anthony Burgess, and Malcolm McDowell trumped my juvenile apprehensions. I wanted very much to see the film.

In Southern California, I would have been ejected from the line had I tried to get into a showing of *A Clockwork Orange*. Just another troublemaking kid thinking he could fool the authorities. My height would have been no cover. Without a well-crafted fake ID, I was doomed.

But in London, the box office person took my money without as much as a skeptical glance. The ushers waived me through with a smile, even showed our little group —

three other guys, all under 18 — to our seats. The staff ignored my sweet, boyish face, which at that time hadn't even sprouted peach fuzz. (I wouldn't start shaving for another three years.) When I got home, I expounded on the merits of the film to my parents, like a budding Truffaut.

*   *   *

I saw many Maple Leaf flag insignias during our six months in London. They were sewn on shirts, jackets, the rear pockets of blue jeans, and backpacks. I initially took this to be simply a collective, public expression of Canadian pride, but my father offered a different interpretation. The true motive, he explained to me, is that Canadians don't want to be mistaken for their neighbors to the south, who were responsible for the war in Vietnam, racism, Richard Nixon, and George Wallace. To the untrained English ear, the Canadian accent sounded quite similar to the American accent, and vice versa. Canadian visitors openly displaying the Maple Leaf wanted to avoid getting hassled by anti-American Brits unable to tell the difference. Love of country was beside the point. The Maple Leaf sent a message to British hosts, "Don't blame me," "It's not our fault," and "We had nothing to do with it."

But I didn't regard the insignias as a necessary act of national self-preservation, and neither did my father, who in fits of pique would refer to Canada as "a shitty little country." I quickly grew irritated at seeing so many displays of the Maple Leaf, day after day, as if London was one big hockey rink. I was deeply offended by the assumption of moral superiority, which seemed to spring from nothing more than the historical fact that their nation was not as big and powerful as my nation. Make Canada responsible for the fate of the Free World, and it would behave just like the United States.

Living in London, I felt protective toward my superpower homeland, and never once tried to hide my roots or accept blatant distortions about my country. I was no more attracted to reflexive anti-Americanism—coming from the British, Canadians, or French—than I was of uncritical patriotism. Both relied on selective marshalling of evidence to arrive at single-minded, simple-minded conclusions. I wondered if it had been like this for Americans living in London in 1949, four years after the end of World War II, before Joe McCarthy's witch hunts, which for good reason appalled many in the West. Do anti-American Europeans tie their feelings to current events? Or is their hostility toward the U.S. purely grounded in anecdotal evidence, without the influence of the media? I'm no fan of Ugly Americans either. Hell, I have to live among those people. But I wouldn't consider them to be representative of the whole, any more than I would regard diffident British visitors I might encounter in Los Angeles as typical of their homeland.

By coincidence, in the year following our sojourn to England, 1972–1973, I did become close friends with a guy from Winnipeg whose family had moved to Southern California. He didn't wear a Maple Leaf on his sweater, but many times took the opportunity to point out the awful things my native country, his now-adopted country, were doing around the world. I couldn't justify the bombing of North Vietnam, although I did object when he drew parallels to the conduct of the Luftwaffe. My fallback strategy during these arguments was to champion the cause of the French-speaking residents of Quebec. I had read just enough to attempt to draw comparisons with the treatment of Blacks and Native Americans in the United States.

*   *   *

One of the great joys of living abroad was reading the *International Herald Tribune*, a combined publication of *The New York Times* and *The Washington Post*. I initially was attracted to the IHT because it was the only place I knew of in the United Kingdom where I could get daily scores from Major League Baseball and the National Basketball Association. Seeking out the sports pages, I started to pay attention to other parts of the paper. It was the IHT that introduced me to the Washington media establishment. I read the major pundits: Joseph Alsop, Jack Anderson, Russell Baker, James Reston, and Tom Wicker, and stories written by David Broder, R.W. Apple, and Sydney Schanberg. I first learned of the Watergate break-in from a piece filed by two *Post* reporters whose names you know.

Reading the IHT, I felt that I was finally receiving the political education that I deserved. By the middle of our stay in London, I was as eager to catch up on Baker and Reston as I was to find out whether my Lakers had defeated the Bucks or the Knicks.

Being a daily consumer of the IHT and a regular viewer of the BBC (the Beeb) turned me into a budding intellectual version of a political junkie. I watched a French television special (with subtitles) about Henry Kissinger, a two-hour program on the militarization of China, and lengthy segments about the Common Market and NATO, among many other topics.

In July, the Beeb's opening day coverage of the 1972 Democratic National Convention included a discussion with William F. Buckley and John Kenneth Galbraith. I was familiar with Buckley—we watched his weekly program *Firing Line* regularly back home—but not Galbraith. The participants had an amiable, literate face-off on such issues as Nixon versus McGovern, Republicans versus Democrats, and Yale versus Harvard.

My politics were much more closely aligned with Galbraith's, but I wouldn't have minded being either of those guys, who were obviously enjoying each other's company immensely. And, yes, it's impossible for me to recall that segment, which lasted maybe 15 minutes, and not think about the cretins who star on present-day, right-wing radio and television. It's like comparing the Rolling Stones to Poison.

In mid-August, my family left the country of Edward Heath, and returned to the country of Richard Nixon. I had closely followed Watergate in the seven weeks since the break-in and monitored the progress of the "secret plan" to end the War in Vietnam, which was now almost four years beyond its expected unveiling. Still, nothing could have prepared me—or I would submit, millions of others older and smarter than me—for what Nixon would put us through over the next two years.

CHAPTER 9

"Rock the Boat"

The Hues Corporation, 1974

I have not attended any of my high school reunions to date, but it's a good bet I'll be at the 50th in 2024. I knew people in the Class of 1974, but my closest friends were members of the Class of 1973 or the Class of 1975. Still, I will look forward to catching up with old acquaintances, reliving our experiences from the age of dial phones to the era of texts and TikTok.

Unfortunately, 1974 is regarded by many as one of the worst in the history of rock and roll. Great songs were essentially nonexistent, good songs were all too rare, and the bad songs were horrible in a way not heard since Bobby Goldsboro's "Honey" six years earlier.

I hope the entertainment committee leaves "Seasons in the Sun," "Billy Don't Be a Hero," and "The Night Chicago Died" off the playlist. If they asked me, I might suggest as rock and roll alternatives "Radar Love," "Come and Get Your Love," and Grand Funk's cover of the "Locomotion." But for the most part, the pop gods went on holiday in 1974.

Say what you will about the trauma of 1968 or the turbulence of 1969, they represented the pinnacle of Top 40 genius, great years to be graduating from high school.

In later years, when I had moved beyond self-pity and gained perspective, I understood the problem. The year 1974 served as a transition between boogie bands and punk/New Wave, commercial funk and disco. Listeners had a sense of the old and familiar but little indication of what was poised to take its place. My senior year experienced more than its fair share of filler pop songs while the mammoth music industry searched frantically for game-saving trends.

I earlier referenced great songs, a few of them, which on reflection seem like miracles because they finished high on the charts in such an awful year: "Radar Love," "Beach Baby," "Who Do You Think You Are" (Bo Donaldson and the Heywoods' unlikely follow up to "Billy Don't be a Hero") and my personal favorite single from 1974, "Rock the Boat," by the Hues Corporation.

I have since heard "Rock the Boat" described as disco, although the term didn't exist at the time of its ascension to pop heaven. "Rock the Boat" is one of those uncommon singles in which every element works to perfection. The commanding piano chords at the opening—sustained throughout—the welcoming horn intro, the smooth, sassy rhythm section, and the gender-blended vocals, in which the female and two males sound like they are singing to respective lovers out there in space: Three distinct relationships on the verge of going under.

The song went to #1, much-needed confirmation that Young America still possessed a tinge of integrity. Although "Rock the Boat" was a plea for stability, it reigned during the final unnerving weeks of the Nixon presidency. Not a problem for me. I loved the song and rooted for the president's impeachment.

       *   *   *

In the early 1970s, class clowns at my high school would do imitations of the then-current president, before small and private audiences of no more than, say, five. One guy would attempt to replicate Nixon's deep-throated tone and proclaim, "Let me say this about that." Others would go for the obvious; goofy grin and extended arms, fingers making the "V for Victory" sign, in imitation of the comic Rich Little's take on Nixon. As the country got deeper into Watergate, the students would be treated to slight variations on "I am not a crook." In those days, Claremont High School could have devoted part of its annual talent show to nothing but Nixon impressions.

On May 17, 1973, I was a few minutes late for school, not a common occurrence. But I had a unique excuse: Nixon made me do it. That morning, at 7 a.m. sharp on the West Coast, the Senate Watergate hearings commenced. My dad was watching on a small portable black and white set in the kitchen, making breakfast. The first witness, some guy involved with the president's re-election committee named Robert Odle, took his seat behind the table. I think he had short hair, pretty sure about that, and wore glasses. His presence wasn't riveting, his style wasn't scintillating, and his testimony wasn't especially revealing. But I wasn't judging Odle on points. I cared only that he was the opening act of what I expected to be a long-running, high-intensity political drama.

Most of the testimony was scheduled for late June and July, when I would be home, looking for entertainment. During the summertime, I bore no resemblance to a classic Southern California boy from the suburbs. I almost never went to the beach, and I never surfed, two facts about me that have not changed in five decades. I loved the Beach Boys and Jan and Dean, but they were not singing about my life.

Because we had been in London for six months in 1972, my family had no plans to go anywhere in the summer of 1973. For the first time, I would have to endure mid-June through Labor Day in Claremont, not an appealing prospect. I had long since stopped playing organized baseball and cut back significantly on pickup games. I had progressed as far as necessary with swimming lessons, and had greatly reduced my candy intake, which kept me amped up during summers in the 60s. As for other vices that might fill the void I was terrified of pot and hated the taste of beer. I didn't even have the rebellious streak or curiosity to become another aimless, rule-breaking suburban teenager.

How many of my straightlaced, nerdish peers around the country were similarly saved by the Watergate hearings? There must be thousands of us, even former and current Republicans, who look back with fondness on that period of history. Even better, I had recently acquired new friends who appealed to me in large part because of their interest in politics. In the past, my main criteria had been the love of sports and war movies. If you owned a leather glove and a plastic gun, we might just have a future together.

Still, for years I had listened to and watched my parents discuss, and in many cases argue about, politics with their friends from academia. By the time I was in high school, it seemed obvious to me that having shared intellectual interests was a critical component of any meaningful relationship. That was in large part how I became friends with Jon, and his brother Joel, plus Sol, and Glenn, at various points during my junior year.

We had all barely missed the traumas of the 1960s, which created a certain generational envy. History had denied us the opportunity to march in the South, protest against the war, campaign for Gene McCarthy or Bobby Kennedy, agonize over whether to avoid the draft. But with Watergate, we could finally follow a major historic event, from start to finish. My new friends and I were absorbed with the details, major and trivial, and took great personal pleasure in knowing something that the other guy did not, including the home states of committee senators, the names of attorneys for the various witnesses, celebrities who made Nixon's Enemies List, and the employers of broadcast and print journalists who covered Watergate. I not only followed the hearings closely for my own enjoyment, I did so to stay even with or ahead of the competition.

In mid-July of 1973, I started to dread the arrival of early August, when the hearings were scheduled to go on hiatus. I would finally be confronted with that awful problem of what to do in the middle of the day when it's 95 degrees outside and the air is unhealthful for even the strongest lungs. Just as I was becoming seriously depressed at the prospect, my dad came to the rescue, and in a most unlikely fashion. He offered me a job, my first.

Well, not my dad exactly, but his employer Harvey Mudd College, at my father's urging. I was hired for the month of August to work with the gardeners and groundskeepers. The position required no experience. Regardless, I knew how to rake leaves, sweep grass, and push a creaky, aging lawn mower.

It was the mechanical devices that posed problems. Since I was a child, I had been alternately terrified of and bored by the prospect of working with my hands. I would occasionally purchase model ships and planes, but they would remain unassembled. Eventually I would pull out the little guns and play my own impromptu war games.

The two full-time gardeners were fine with my work ethic but understandably frustrated by my technical incompetence. Because I was only on staff for a month, we agreed to make the best of it. The only exception was the day that I nearly drove the office electric cart down an open stairwell outside one of the dorms. I turned left inside of right and put the vehicle in reverse when it should have been moving forward. I was riding alone at the time, but word of the incident got back to the head gardener, who wasn't at all pleased. As punishment, I was ordered to spend the rest of the day hoeing and lifting rocks from a bone-dry, caked patch of dirt, with temperatures in the high 90s.

Despite that incident, I ended the month on good terms with my gardening colleagues. Or perhaps they were just glad to see me go. My last day, we listened to radio in the tool shed, turning up the volume for "Brother Louie" by the Stories, the #1 song in America. Although I lived only a few blocks from campus, I never saw those guys again.

The wages allowed me to indulge my growing addiction to politics. I spent much of my salary on one-year subscriptions to the The Nation, The New Republic (TNR), and the Sunday edition of *The Washington Post*, which arrived at my home the following Thursday. I welcomed the paper every week like it was a favorite relative coming to visit. I collected the bulky package, removed the loose-fitting plastic cover, and proceeded to read every word of the "A" section and the opinion pages, as if I would be quizzed on the contents the following day. I didn't feel duped, foolish, or ripped off receiving this first draft of history four days late. It was pure joy to hold in my 17-year-old hands the Sunday edition of *The Washington Post*, then the most famous newspaper in America.

During the Nixon years, TNR moved to the political center, and far to the right of *The Nation*. But the publications were not yet engaged in intellectual civil war. In the early 1970s, however, you could be an avid reader of *The Nation* and *The New Republic* without having to choose sides.

When *The Nation* wrote a lead editorial blasting the conduct of the Los Angeles Police Department during the May 1974 shootout with members of the Symbionese Liberation Army, I pompously proclaimed to my father that I was very seriously considering cancelling my subscription. I believed the SLA members in that house were nothing less than a gang of violent criminals who had gotten what they deserved, annihilation by fire, literally. I couldn't support an official position that blamed the cops for what I considered a just response. My father, who had been through his own share of far left/center left battles, suggested that I not be quite so hasty. Then again, it was my money, and if I wanted to drop *The Nation*, I had the right to do so. After fuming for a few days, I regained my political equilibrium, and decided to continue with the magazine. As a footnote, over the years,

I've come to believe that the harsh criticism of the LAPD in this case was not unreasonable.

I no longer subscribe to *The Nation* or *The New Republic*, although I do peruse the occasional article online. As for *The Washington Post*, I read the electronic version daily, but the advantage of immediacy cannot compete with the high of receiving the gigantic Sunday paper, still smelling of newsprint, the following Thursday at my California address.

*   *   *

My happiest memory from the summer of 1974 is the night that my girlfriend and I watched Nixon's resignation speech. The rest of my family had gone to New Mexico for three weeks that summer, and my parents had left me in charge of the house. Not a big gamble on their part. Other than locking the doors, making sure the pilot light on the stove was turned off, and feeding the cat there wasn't much to the job. As a handyman, I was a complete failure, but I would know whom to call should anything go wrong.

My girlfriend and I didn't exactly cohabitate, but there were a few occasions when she stayed through the night. On the morning of August 8, 1974, her 17th birthday, national media broke the story that Nixon was expected to resign the presidency that evening in his 6 p.m. address (PST) from the Oval Office. In those days, restaurants didn't have television. The two of us couldn't both celebrate her birthday and watch the president announce his intention to quit. But the birthday girl generously offered without hesitation to delay the festivities.

There have been countless stories about where people were, what they were doing, when they received the news from Dallas on November 22, 1963. I even included one of them in this book. But I can't recall a single article or interview in which the subject shared that memory regarding the evening of August 8, 1974, even though Nixon is the only president to ever quit the office. The poor guy has always been second to JFK.

My girlfriend and I sat fully clothed on a bed in my parents' empty house, two politically conscious teenagers in love, excited and nervous to watch the final moments of an ignominious presidency. Setting friskiness aside, our complete focus on the screen, it felt to me like we were a young, married couple, engaged citizens concerned about the future of their country.

When one is in the throes of a first romance, pretend marriage has a strong allure, a utopian promise of permanence, maturity, and, as a dopey male coworker once said to me, "ass every night." Both M and I were ambitious, middle-class kids; college was in the offing. Getting married would have to wait—if it happened at all. I would be heading east in a few weeks, to Brandeis University in Waltham, Massachusetts, an industrial and academic town, and she would be starting her senior year of high school, with hopes of attending UC Irvine. We had made vague pledges of fidelity, and talked about marriage in the abstract, but that night was as close as we ever came. Still, as the two of us expectantly awaited Nixon's address, it seemed as if we were Mr. and Ms.

CHAPTER 10

"Get Off of My Cloud"

The Rolling Stones, 1965

In the fall of my senior year in high school, I was home and completely alone on a Saturday night—even my younger brother and sister had something to do, somewhere to go. Although I was sufficiently removed from the Claremont High School social scene not to brood over my hapless circumstances, I did feel bored and restless, a middle-class, teenage cliché. I tried watching television, flipping from one channel to the next, nothing but trite sitcoms and sterile crime dramas. I switched to books and magazines, but it was impossible to concentrate. I pulled an issue of *Playboy* out of the closet—I had hidden it there myself—and turned to the centerfold, a blonde no less. Even though Hef had added pubic hair to the portraits, I looked at the young lady, shrugged, and set the magazine aside. The problem was not her, but me.

Thoroughly disengaged, operating on adolescent autopilot, I drifted into the room that contained the extremely modest record collection that my brother and I had assembled over the previous seven years. Most of the albums had been purchased between 1966 and 1971, before my interest in Top 40 hits and album rock waned. Even in England, the country that introduced me to David Bowie and T. Rex on *Top of the Pops,* I didn't purchase a single LP.

I was preparing to vacate the area, aimlessly seek another diversion, when I noticed an album by the Rolling Stones entitled *December's Children.* Released at the end of 1965, it had been given to us by a friend of my brother's, who preferred the Stones to the Beatles, a rarity among elementary school kids I knew in the 1960s. I looked at the cover and was instantly intrigued by a black and white photo that depicted five somber guys staring at us through what appeared to be an extremely narrow doorway. The image was bleak, sparse, and cold, perpetuating the always appealing pop culture myth of "us" against the world.

I had been too young to appreciate or understand the transition from rock and roll to rock, singles to albums, screaming girls to stoned humanities majors. I knew the after, but not the before. I didn't get the joke on the *Sgt. Pepper* cover when the "new" Beatles bid farewell to the mop tops.

But now I was 17, an aspiring intellectual, who read *The Nation* and *The New Republic* and discussed Hegel with my father. In a few months I would attempt, unsuccessfully, to tackle the entire *Ulysses.* I was also a horny high school kid — the ideal rock and roll fan — who didn't want to be only known as a horny high school kid. I insisted on being taken seriously, appreciated for my mind, by rock groups and anyone else.

I turned the album over, read the liner notes. The Stones' manager, Andrew Loog Oldham, the guy forever known in pop culture circles for having the brilliant insight to market his clients as smug, vulgar, and violence-prone, had written several lines of hipster verse that attempted to place the album within its contemporary political and social context. His words were intended to lower expectations among the politically engaged members of the audience that the Stones were preparing to lead the revolution. Oldham wrote that the group's music had no answers to "the sea of faces" regarding the "riots in downtown LA," the war in "uptown Vietnam," or "who killed that prince of peace in Dallas a year or so ago." Don't expect Mick Jagger and Keith Richards, rhythm and blues fanatics and burgeoning pop songwriters, to make sense of the confusing, chaotic, frightening world of 1965.

I read this pseudo-poem in late 1973, months after President Nixon had brought the last American troops home from South Vietnam and all of the U.S. POWs had been freed from prisons in North Vietnam. White people were still afraid to go to Watts, but the riots had occurred more than eight years earlier. I didn't need the Stones or any other rock and roll band to guide me through turbulent times. The nation was in the midst of Watergate, but who would want to record a pop song about a complex political scandal? (In 1974, after Nixon resigned, Lynyrd Skynyrd released the hit "Sweet Home Alabama," which included the famous lyric "Watergate does not bother me." That was pretty much the extent of rock's response.) Yet, I felt a rising sense of excitement reading the liner notes, instantly transported back to the political trauma of the 1960s. That, and the alluring album jacket made me long for the era in a way I never had before.

After this buildup, I had to play the record. I went into the living room, removed the plastic lid covering the turntable. It had been a long time since I used my dad's stereo system, the only one in the house. I checked the settings and adjusted the bass and the volume to levels appropriate for the occasion. I glanced at the song list: "Get Off of My Cloud," first track on side two. The title seemed familiar but I didn't recall the sound. Fast or medium tempo? Big beat or blues groove? Guitar solo or repeated chords?

I put needle to vinyl, heard a few bumps and pops, and then the opening. Charlie Watts, the Stones' drummer, did the honors: Two thunderous "booms" on the tom-tom followed by the shooting sparks of a snare drum roll. Mick Jagger let out an appreciative "yeah," and away they went. A few minutes earlier, I was a lonely boy slouched on a chair, desperately in search of diversions. Now I was accompanying the one and only Rolling Stones on air drums and air guitar. When "Get Off Of My Cloud" ended, I raised the needle, and returned it to the beginning of the album. I continued this routine for another 15 minutes.

The rest of the LP did not equal the majesty of the opening song but was deeply satisfying nonetheless. On *December's Children*, the Stones were experimenting, in a limited mid-60s way, with various "hit" sounds. The album featured ballads, including "As Tears Go By," blues, mid-tempo pop, and a couple of superfast numbers, the Ramones a decade before the Ramones.

I had a few previous encounters with the Rolling Stones, although none that seemed noteworthy at the time. In the summer of 1967, my brother was friends with a bad boy who smoked cigarettes in fifth grade and was showing an unhealthy interest in more potent stuff. He gave us a copy of the Rolling Stones album, *12 × 5*, which was released a few months prior to *December's Children*. My mom saw my brother and me looking at the album and offered an impromptu opinion of a kind I had never heard from her before. "Oh god, the Rolling Stones, yuck," said this woman, who had graduated from Swarthmore. "They are so disgusting." At that point, I knew nothing about the group, including the name of the lead singer. Unlike the Monkees, whose honor I would immediately defend, I didn't have any loyalty to the Rolling Stones. I let my mother speak her piece without offering any resistance.

A few years later, my brother received *Sticky Fingers* for his 13th birthday. He played it repeatedly for a couple of weeks. I liked several of the tracks, especially "Wild Horses" and "Brown Sugar," but I didn't buy the hype, World's Greatest Rock and Roll Band.

But on that Saturday night in December, a few weeks after Richard Nixon fired Special Prosecutor Archibald Cox and others in the Saturday Night Massacre, I went from being an intermittent rock and roll fan to an obsessive. It started with the Rolling Stones, but soon seeped into all areas of 1960s rock. Over the next year, my record collection expanded over several shelves. I mostly purchased greatest hits packages: The Animals, the Byrds, the Hollies, the Turtles, the Who, and so on. Once a month, I would drive with friends from Claremont to the famous Tower Records store on Sunset Boulevard, 40 miles to the west, and stock up on LPs, five at a time.

I assembled a rock and roll library as well, purchasing paperback anthologies of record reviews, interviews, and feature stories that had originally been published in *Rolling Stone*. I bought any book about the Rolling Stones or the Beatles that I could find, plus others that covered the entire history of the genre, or particular periods and places. When I entered bookstores, I no longer first visited the history section, but headed straight to music. I was as attracted to rock journalism as I was to rock, which in my mind complemented each other perfectly. It was the beginning of a creative interest that continues unabated.

Being home alone on a Saturday night can be a godsend.

CHAPTER 11

"Purple People Eater"

Sheb Wooley, 1958

I was at home on a weekday afternoon, either because school had let out early or my last class had been cancelled, I don't recall. A guy in his late 30s and his helper son were in the kitchen, fixing the washer and dryer. The man worked while listening on his electric radio to LA station KRTH, which played nothing but hit records from 1955 to the end of 1963, just before the Beatles came to America. The son, probably in high school, seemed embarrassed by his dad's taste in music. He shook his head and looked down at the floor when the old man sang along to "Purple People Eater" by Sheb Wooley.

I agreed that "Purple People Eater" sounded ridiculous, but not most of the other artists, songs, and genres KRTH programmed that day, including Chuck Berry, Fats Domino, Little Richard, Del Shannon, the Dovells, and Doo Wop.

I had grown up during the height of 1960s and 1970s liberal arrogance, when the 1950s was frequently portrayed as the nadir of American culture and politics; racism, sexism, homophobia, Joe McCarthy, schlock, paranoia, a terrible fashion sense, and the harboring of weird secrets. According to the left-wing company line, in the decade before enlightenment arrived, America was suffocating under the weight of its own repression. Mocking the 1950s had become a cottage industry; all those silly virgin girls and comically naïve boys, hair dripping of Brylcreem, stranger than any invaders from outer space.

It was a half-truth, at best, but I didn't have the knowledge or frankly the interest to advocate on behalf of the accused. I went along with the standard account, including a blanket dismissal of early rock and roll. Until the repairman turned on the oldies station, I had probably heard a total of 25 rock and roll songs released in the 1950s, most of them from the soundtrack of the hit film *American Graffiti*, which I had seen a few months earlier. I loved the movie, yet I didn't care enough about the music to mourn what I had missed.

After the worker and his son left, I switched the dial on my paint-spattered clock radio to KRTH, where it remained for weeks. I had a new era to explore, which would require considerable time and research. While my high school class-mates were listening to Black Sabbath, Pink Floyd, Alice Cooper, and Deep Purple, I was learning the lyrics to "Diana," "Duke of Earl," and "Denise," and loudly practicing the verbal pyrotechnics that opened the Marcels' cover of "Blue Moon."

My tastes were unmistakably retro, yet I felt that I was the cool one. Any high school student can listen to what's hot at the moment. No risk in that. But I was digging the 50s, of all decades, a period in rock and roll and social history that few of my peers took seriously, and some despised. Still, I was not willing to openly press the case or endure teasing and ridicule to demonstrate my uniqueness. Walking the hallways of Claremont High School, I looked like the average early 70s male student: bushy long hair, blue jeans, athletic shoes manufactured by Adidas or Converse. No one except close friends knew of my secret. In their presence, however, I was a tireless advocate, daring them to deny that the sax opening to "Diana" was pure musical genius, or insisting that they acknowledge that the "Rhythm of the Rain" by the Cascades, a San Diego group, was the British Invasion before the British Invasion.

Although I was the only member of my little group with such an all-consuming interest, I did have an ally, my friend, Pete Sanders, a massive Buddy Holly fan. He owned a two-record set of Holly's greatest hits, on the MCA label, which he played constantly, often providing running commentary alongside the songs. Apart from "That'll Be the Day," which I loved, I couldn't name a single Holly song when I began my journey through 1950s rock and roll. Listening to Pete's album, I was astounded by Holly's composition skills, switching effortlessly from rock and roll to rhythm and blues to soft ballads to country twang to nascent folk rock in the song "Well....All Right." It was the same material John and Paul heard when they began as songwriters. In his range and virtuosity, Buddy Holly seemed like a composer from the 60s, to me still the highest form of flattery.

As noted, I had, without thinking, absorbed the low regard in which elites held the 1950s. But after listening to KRTH for several months, to the general exclusion of album rock and 60s hits, I wondered: Can an era that produced so many great songs and performers be so bad? If Chuck Berry was hugely popular in the 50s, didn't that say something good about the decade? I started to closely examine the social history of the period from 1955–1963, working my way past hula hoops, college pranks, and snide references to *Father Knows Best* and *Ozzie and Harriet* to what I hoped would be a deeper understanding.

Starting at typical photos of middle-class 1950s youth, freckled-faced guys in short hair and white t-shirts and girls with skirts down to their ankles, I found it difficult to shake the stereotype of complacency and innocence. I couldn't imagine these kids losing their minds over Little Richard or storming the stage at a Jerry Lee Lewis concert. I believed that Ike-era kids tacitly if not aggressively supported the prevailing politics of the time, which I interpreted as virulently anti-Soviet, racially insensitive if not racist, and strongly committed to dad goes to work, mom cleans the house and raises the children, the traditional gender roles. This was an obvious exaggeration; yet, I couldn't get beyond the buzz cuts. I had spent most of my young political life associating guys like that with Nixon and George Wallace.

But my unlikely passion for early rock and roll and R&B forced me to confront my own intellectual biases and hasty judgments about the 1950s. Influenced by the music, I re-examined the politics of the decade and concluded that things were not as simple as snooty critics had suggested. The Montgomery Bus Boycott, which occurred in 1955, launched the Civil Rights Movement. Joe McCarthy had terrorized America in the early 50s. He was censured by his Senate colleagues in 1954, the year of Rock Around the Clock. He died in disgrace three years later. The Korean War ended in 1953, the same year that Hugh Hefner introduced *Playboy*. It began to make sense — so many great artists and songs came out of the second half of the decade, one of the most fertile periods in the history of American pop culture, a much-needed break from a series of traumatic events.

CHAPTER 12

Beyond The Valley of the Dolls

Russ Meyer, 1970

This chapter, unlike the others, is not named for a song, but an X-rated film that I became obsessed with in the eighth grade, yet not for the reasons you would expect.

A junior high school English teacher told our class on several occasions that *Sex and the Single Girl* was the classic example of a book that became hugely popular solely on the basis of its brilliantly suggestive title. I took her word for it, although at the time I knew very little about single girls and even less about sex. I still haven't read the book, but I have read quite a bit about its author, the late Helen Gurley Brown, the editor of *Cosmopolitan*, who had sex with many different men before that form of recreation become more common. I continue to idolize sexually liberated women, especially if they had their fun before the official onset of the sexual revolution. They flouted double standards and sexist rules about female sexual conduct in a way that I found beguiling.

Sex and the Single Girl may not have done much for me, but I was enthralled with the title *Beyond the Valley of the Dolls*, released in the summer of 1970, between eighth and ninth grade. Part of that was its juxtaposition with real events. In August 1969, Sharon Tate, star of *Valley of the Dolls*, was murdered with four others at a mansion in the hills above Los Angeles. At the time, my family and I were on vacation in Vancouver, Canada. When the news came over the radio, my mother exclaimed "What?!" because the story made no sense, even after so many other events that made little sense since the Cuban Missile Crisis. It made less sense four months later, when Charles Manson and many members of his family were arrested for the murders. By the time *Beyond the Valley of the Dolls* was released, Manson and four of his followers were on trial for the killings. With each revelation, the story got more bizarre, a series of crimes that could only have been committed in the late 1960s.

As noted before, during my adolescent years I was afraid of X-rated films, which like horror movies suggested to me a creepy, sordid, grotesque underworld of hideous acts vividly displayed on screen. In my case, the daunting "X" served its purpose, blunting any curiosity I might have about the contents. Still, I was growing up at a time when X-rated films were being released and advertised at a rate of several per month. I couldn't help but notice them as I scanned the movie ads for more respectable faire.

Beyond the Valley of the Dolls (which I have never seen to this day) primarily caught my attention because of the title. And, it was about an all-female rock and roll group, a rarity in the 1960s and 70s. But it also came out a month or so after I saw my first college-aged, fully nude woman, under circumstances that would never occur today. I unwittingly participated in the Sexual Revolution years before I had actual sex.

In Claremont, my family lived just northwest of Scripps College, an esteemed institution for women founded in 1926. The campus in the late 1960s radiated a kind of serene beauty: cool, green fields occupied by male and female students flirting, lone students sleeping or studying, elms with rubbery trunks alongside sturdy oaks and sycamores, narrow paths, flanked by hedges and flowers, dorms that projected midcentury elegance and style. As with Pomona College a few blocks away, out-of-state visitors gazed at Scripps and wondered how such a charming and lovely campus was located in soulless, smoggy Southern California.

One Sunday afternoon in the late spring of 1970, my friends and I were approached at Scripps by a male student, carrying a small movie camera, who asked if he could borrow a few of us for a moment. An unusual request, but what kid in Southern California can resist an offer to appear on camera? He walked our group to a spot several yards away. A woman wearing a loose, white jumper and no shoes lay flat on the grass. She looked to be around 19, had her arms at her side, and was staring skyward, apparently oblivious to the pack of young male strangers invading her space. She was soft, pretty, and seemed friendly, the kind of woman I would never have approached on my own at 13 — or 17, for that matter.

The filmmaker lined us up and issued simple instructions: lift the jumper, one by one, peer inside, react to the camera. Like a good extra, I did as I was told, noticing her smooth, endless skin. Did all college-age women, I wondered, go out in public without any underwear? Did all women, period, go out in public without wearing any underwear?

I did not actually see what I was supposed to see. I was too timid to look further. I observed the woman's bare thighs, rising to a point, but didn't get the full view, which may have been the intent of the avant garde aspirant with the camera.

I stared into the lens and gave the requested wide-eyed response. In reality, I was more confused than aroused, no offense to the model. When the five of us "actors" traded notes, it turned out that a couple of guys thought they noticed a mound of soft, brown hair; then again, maybe not. Junior high school boys are not known for their intimate understanding of the female body.

Throughout the entire episode, the "actress" remained quiet and still. Her silence seemed strange, but on the other hand, words would have been superfluous, potentially turning this attempt at art house erotica into comedy. I can only surmise her instructions were to show up, play the part, and have no interaction with the supporting cast. We never found out her name, her age, or connection to Scripps, if any.

I never learned what happened to this so-called film, although for obvious reasons I'll never forget it. Her apparent consent to having pre- and barely teen male virgins view her pubic hair was in line with recent changes in American social mores. I would learn that starting in the mid-1960s, college-aged women were on average having more sex or much more sex than prior generations. Glancing at this impassive model, it didn't appear she was enjoying the new freedoms. Men were still dictating the terms based on what *they* desired. The woman might have preferred taking a nap that hazy afternoon, alone in her room, with or without clothes.

CHAPTER 13

"Do It Baby"

The Miracles, 1974

In most of the Baby Boomer memoirs I've read, the sexual awakening begins in college, if it happens at all. But during my entire freshman year at Brandeis University, I did not so much as kiss a member of either sex, which also would not seem out of place in a Hollywood film about the 1950s or 1960s.

For the first few months away, I was gripped with an extreme case of homesickness. I missed my girlfriend and Southern California, plus I compounded my misery by making little or no effort to meet other students. I often took the short train ride to Cambridge, wandering the streets around Harvard alone and sad, in conscious though inaccurate imitation of the great thinkers that had traveled those hallowed paths before me. Unfortunately, in my case suffering did not spur creativity.

But I eventually emerged from my antisocial cocoon, both because I grudgingly accepted my circumstances and because I became curious about these people I saw on campus every day.

At that time, the nation had not adopted a universal standard for underage drinking. I had left a state where the age was 21 for a state where one could legally drink at 18. On August 24, 1974, I turned 18; four days later, I flew from Los Angeles to Boston.

It wouldn't have made a whit of difference to me if the drinking age in Massachusetts was 25. I didn't like the taste of beer, and I was not so desperate for male credibility or female attention that I drank brew just for the sake of it. But a lower drinking age didn't just allow me to purchase alcohol at the corner liquor store if I were so inclined. It also meant that my fellow freshmen and I could spend Saturday nights at the campus pub.

It was there that I learned to dance, or I should just say "danced," since I wasn't very good. I twitched more than I moved, placed the onus on the wrong body parts. But we went as a group, girls and guys, and the collective enjoyment of getting on the floor whenever a popular song came over the jukebox outweighed any embarrassment I may have felt. There were a lot of musical options, with funk and now disco competing for young America's attention.

I actually got pretty good at a simple step called "The Bump," which involved coordinating modest pelvic thrusts in time with your partner. The song that we bumped to the most was "Do It Baby" by the Miracles, which had a perfect double beat at the end of each phrase. Smokey Robinson and the Miracles had been my favorite Motown group, not even close, and when the lead singer/composer/most famous member departed, I presumed that the remaining members had no chance. In my opinion, it didn't make sense for the Miracles to continue.

I wouldn't have even known about "Do It Baby" if not for Saturday nights at the campus pub. I was listening exclusively to hard rock stations at the time. But whenever the song was played, we set down our plastic cups of beer, took a break from table gossip, and headed for the cramped dance floor. Along with the double beat, the number included a part where the instruments stopped and the lead vocalist sang "Do it, do it, do it, ya." Once again, Motown had come up with an ideal hook, which resisted all attempts to banish it from the mind. Members of our pub group would sometimes greet each other out in public by singing, "Do it, do it, do it, ya."

"Do It Baby" not only reached #1, and deservedly so, it was better than the stuff the Miracles released with Smokey over the previous couple of years. Unfortunately, the newer version could not sustain the momentum. The group had another big hit a few months later with a song called "Love Machine," but that one was a typical disco blitz, different from and inferior to the cool groove of "Do it Baby." By the late 1970s, the Miracles had started to fade. In the spring of 1980, Smokey released a solo single called "Cruisin'," which we couldn't keep in stock at Tower Records in West Covina, California. The Miracles had succeeded without him, now he was succeeding without them, and Motown was the beneficiary in both cases.

*   *   *

At Brandeis, my roommate was Catholic; I was half-Jewish, and everyone else in our 16-guy suite was fully Jewish. On the wall over his bed, my roommate placed a woodcut representation of Christ on the cross. He claimed to do so for reasons of faith, and not to provoke his suitemates. Nobody asked him to take it down, although on occasion a few of us would regard the figure with mild disgust or mock horror. I once made a snide reference to "your friend on the cross," but that was more a feeble attempt at pagan humor than an actual insult. Another guy in the suite, a liberal on most issues, pinned a Confederate flag over his bed. He said it was a universal symbol of "defiance against authority." It's a tough call, but I would rather go to bed every night seeing Christ on the cross than a Confederate flag.

That first week, a budding musician at the end of our suite played a side of *Hot Rocks*, the Rolling Stones' double album of greatest hits. Hearing "19th Nervous Breakdown" jolted me out of what was already creeping homesickness, mixed with pangs of puppy love. I regarded the album as an invitation, visited his room, and introduced myself. His name was Doug, he played bass, and we became close friends for the year. We once spent an entire afternoon in a good-natured debate over who was the superior musician, Jimmy Page (my choice) or Jack Bruce (his). Doug put a "Do Not Disturb" sign on his door, and we proceeded to have a song-against-song face off, playing tracks from various albums to demonstrate versatility and virtuosity. At the end, we agreed to disagree and proclaimed the competition a draw.

I don't know exactly when liberal arts colleges adopted a laissez-faire attitude about drugs in dorms. At Brandeis I learned that unwritten rule understood by students and authorities. It wasn't exactly an open market in our suite, but joints or pot-filled pipes were usually close at hand. Although I never saw people drop acid, I saw its effects. LSD scared me, for the same reason as tall, winding roller coasters. I didn't need to add total loss of control to my list of existential crises.

When I was there, Brandeis set aside one entire day and a few nights for campus bacchanalias. We figured these events were a holdover from 60s hedonism without realizing that youth culture was now fully immersed in 70s hedonism. One party I attended was called "Usdan Lives," in honor of the student center where it took place. The ambience was late 60s: rock bands, strobe lights, cigarettes, and doobies. During a break in the music, organizers projected a series of porn shorts on a large wall for all of us to see, males and females together. One I recall involved a thin, pale young woman having intercourse on a table with Batman and Robin, who except for their very visible penises remained in costume the entire time.

I suspect the majority of Brandeis students had never viewed porn in the company of so many of their peers. While the film was being projected, I was aware of people looking at the wall, yet acting like they were not, intense curiosity with staged indifference. We were not a porn generation, but a generation coming into porn, unsure how to behave in its distracting presence. *Playboy* and *Penthouse* had not properly prepared us for watching people actually having sex, in various machinations. Indeed, compared with porn's clumsy production values and working-class milieu, on and off screen, those glossy magazines seemed elitist, remote, just one more unattainable Hollywood fantasy. Bob Guccione and Hugh Hefner would never have associated their publishing empires with anything so grubby and amateurish as Batman and Robin having sex with a young woman who was not centerfold material. But in those pioneering days, class division was part of porn's appeal: low-budget romps that revealed bloat in the pleasure industry.

The morning after the screening, a coed from Philadelphia named Heidi asked me what I thought of the film. Even in my innocent youth, I knew that a young man had to be careful discussing porn with a young woman. Enthusiasm could be construed as a personal insult, and a sign of incurable sexism. On the other hand, a noncommittal response would seem like a lie, told solely for the purpose of exiting an uncomfortable conversation as quickly as possible.

I chose a third option, which was not half bad, under duress. Adopting a thoughtful tone, searching for just the right words, I told Heidi that the film "took something beautiful..." Before I could finish, she added, "and made it cheap." I nodded in agreement. The two of us had arrived at a mutually satisfying assessment. Heidi seemed pleased with my mature response. I passed the test.

Did I believe it? Not so much. I was too new to sex and overwhelmed by its implications, beginning with naked man climbs into bed with naked woman, to think of it as "beautiful." Still, I was certainly no libertine, willing to argue passionately in support of the notion of "sex for sex's sake." Although I was consumed with lust at that age, I couldn't comprehend that people might simply sleep with each other for one night or a long weekend. What was the etiquette involved in setting up these arrangements? Did the man ask the woman, "Would you like to spend the night at my place?" Or did the woman take the lead because that's how it worked in the 70s? Either way, my tightly wound personality would prevent me from being in these situations. That's how I felt anyway. I certainly never asked any coed at Brandeis if she would like to go to bed, nor did I receive such an offer.

*   *   *

As the proud owner of a laptop, I have watched many hours of erotica and porn since viewing that short involving Batman, Robin, and a very willing woman. Like all successful business ventures, the content has expanded to meet the increasing demands of its clientele. In the 2020s, the connoisseur and novice can both expect to have even their peculiar preferences satisfied; if not, there's probably an online suggestion box where the viewer can propose story lines. The adult industry seems accommodating to its audience, whoever and wherever they may be.

Yet, aside from purchasing adult magazines now and then—in the 1980s and 1990s, long before I bought the laptop —and renting the occasional soft core film when I was in a hotel room, alone and feeling lazy—my only other monetary contribution to the industry was one visit to a strip club.

It was a cloudy Monday afternoon in the early 2000s, and I was driving from Los Angeles to San Diego on business. I decided somewhere around San Clemente that today I would finally do it, get up the courage to enter one of those dark establishments that had tempted me for years with the promise of "Nude Girls." I had done some research and learned that there was just such a place located in an industrial area maybe 20 miles from downtown San Diego. With shaky hands, but feeling really good about myself, I exited the freeway, turned onto a side street, and parked the car directly in front of the entrance.

My first impression walking through the door was that Monday afternoons were not income generators for strip clubs. There was one guy in attendance, sitting quietly a few feet from the stage, apparently waiting for the next performance. A comely brunette wearing a friendly smile and white lingerie came around to take our drink orders: soda, juice, or water. I learned from the program that she had been something of a success on the "nude circuit," having won various awards: One more reminder that under capitalism you can make a career out of just about anything.

Some 15 minutes later the music started, a thumping cross between techno and disco, and from behind the curtain emerged a blonde woman in her late 20s or early 30s, wearing only a G-string and heels. She swung around the pole a couple of times, discarding her few items of clothing in the process. At this point I got nervous, not because I was in close proximity to a nude woman, but because I was ignorant of strip club etiquette. How was I supposed to show my appreciation? Applaud? Whistle? Dance in the aisles? Luckily, the other guy was a veteran. He opened his wallet, removed a $20 bill, and flipped it on to the stage. Not a minute later I opened my wallet, removed a $20 bill, and flipped it on to the stage. I did not have all that much cash with me, and as a person who perpetually worried about money, was not prepared to continue this practice much longer, regardless of how exquisite the performance.

The dancer, perhaps sensing my parsimonious inclinations, in a loud voice let the audience of two know that "Today is my birthday." Being gentlemen, we responded with "Happy Birthday," each of us tossing another $20 bill on to the glittering platform. It was not until hours later, in my hotel room, when I became suspicious. Many of the women I know don't go to work on their birthdays. Yet this charming lady, a part-time stripper, chose to report for duty on hers, which that year fell on a Monday? Oh, well, it was only an extra $20.

CHAPTER 14

"War"

Edwin Starr, 1970

The first time I heard Edwin Starr's "War," in the summer of 1970, I didn't immediately think of it as an antiwar song with an ironic title. I was drawn to the single's finger-pointing lyrics, incensed vocals, industrial rhythm, bone-rattling sax, and fluid, aggressive guitar riffs. The entire production sounded like an angry student leader speaking through a bullhorn at a massive protest.

"War" was not explicitly about Vietnam, although it was impossible to avoid making that connection in the summer of 1970, a mere four months after Richard Nixon ordered the invasion of Cambodia. It certainly occurred to me, a 14-year-old who couldn't remember a time before the War in Vietnam. I first started picking up bits of information about the war from the television news broadcasts my parents watched in the mid-1960s. By late 1967, when I started reading the front page of the newspaper, both the war and the huge demonstrations it spawned were a daily part of my political education.

When "War" came out, the only other antiwar song I knew was Country Joe's "I-Feel-Like-I'm-Fixin'-to-Die," which was explicitly about Vietnam. Still, I was the eldest child in an academic family, and we lived in Berkeley during two of the most tumultuous years of the war, a time when Walter Cronkite declared on the *CBS Evening News* that the United States couldn't win over there. I was aware of the war, every day of my youth.

In the summer of 1967, my family and I went to an antiwar potluck at a three-story, wood-framed house in Claremont with a large backyard. The host, director of the theater department at Pomona College, had invited hundreds of academics, students, and performers of various kinds. There were speeches, an auction to raise money for some worthy cause or causes associated with the antiwar movement, and live theater. A folk-rock group called The South performed (its tagline was "The South is Rising," perhaps not the most appropriate association for this crowd). My brother and I spent the night at the home; the guitarist for the South came upstairs and played a few songs for us — including "Hit the Road, Jack" — on his acoustic while we grew ever more tired and eventually fell asleep. When John and I arrived home the next morning my mother said she regretted allowing us to stay there. With all those smokers on the premises, she explained, the entire house could have burst into flames at any moment.

In October 1969, my family and I attended an antiwar rally at Pomona College, part of the national moratorium day. Along with hundreds of others, we sat in the dust of a well-worn football field as various speakers riffed on the theme that the United States must withdraw from Vietnam, achieve peace now. I agreed with the message, especially since Nixon was president, and no one in my family trusted him on anything. Still, I expected the war to continue, because it had been going on for most of my childhood, and I couldn't fathom that it might end. I knew from history that wars do in fact end, but in 1943 did the average 13-year-old feel that World War II would eventually come to a halt? Or, what about an eighth-grader in 1916, when trench war was at its peak? Was he or she confident that the slaughter would run its course, and soon?

"My war" eventually came to an end, although it gave rise to "The Vietnam Syndrome," which a number of historians and pundits say we are still experiencing nearly 50 years later. But by the time the last Americans departed Saigon in 1975, my views had evolved a bit from the kid who was perfectly in sync with the antiwar movement.

*   *   *

My initial week on the Brandeis campus, I sent the student newspaper, appropriately called *The Justice*, an unsolicited review of a biography of Henry Kissinger written by the television correspondents Bernard and Marvin Kalb. I had never done anything so brash, but at college I felt an immediate need to get noticed. After a few anxious days, the editor called to tell me that the review was excellent, and the paper intended to publish it. The piece ran a few days later. I kept a copy of the article for myself and mailed one to my parents.

My review criticized the book for being too soft on its subject. As one example, the authors had little to say regarding the behind-the-scenes American effort to undermine the elected Marxist leader of Chile, Salvador Allende, who was murdered in a 1973 coup.

Despite my critique, I was far from an unreconstructed liberal/radical on foreign policy issues. Starting in high school, I had become intellectually offended by the tendency of the New Left to condemn all things American and at the same time romanticize America's antagonists, even if those antagonists had a valid argument or cause.

In April 1975, it became increasingly obvious that North Vietnam would capture Saigon (today Ho Chi Minh City) and win the war. Throughout that month the media reported the swift advance of the North Vietnamese army, marching to Saigon, smashing whatever resistance remained. Americans watched with dismay, a sense of resignation, or, in some cases, satisfaction as our former ally succumbed to the inevitable. Before retiring to study in our dorm rooms, various members of my suite would turn on the evening news, usually Walter Cronkite, and follow the steady advance of America's adversary. For those who fervently believed in anti-communism, especially if they served in government or the military, it must have felt like being on a geopolitical death watch.

My suitemates and I did not have such a personal investment in the outcome, but neither were we disinterested observers. Early in the month, three weeks before the last Americans fled Saigon, a number of us had gathered to watch the Academy Awards. The winner for best documentary feature was an antiwar film entitled *Hearts and Minds*. In his acceptance speech, one of the filmmakers proclaimed something to the effect that "Vietnam is now free." I scoffed and said for the entertainment of the others in the room, "Yeah, right, Vietnam is free."

My sarcastic comment drew a quick response from E, who lived three doors down from me. E was quite handsome, and he had a string of girlfriends, each better looking than the one before. One night E brought a young lady into his room, and to accompany or cover whatever activities the couple had planned, he put an Allman Brothers album on the stereo. Whether by accident or design, the LP played on repeat, at high volume, throughout the night. I don't know about E and his friend, but it sure affected my sleep.

About midway through the semester, we bestowed a nickname on E: "Charley." A group of us had been watching a late-night special about the Manson Family murders, when the narrator quoted some deranged remark Charles Manson had made about Hitler and the Jews. E seemed to find Manson's comment quite funny, which was not how the rest of us took it. And so, he became "Charley."

After I passed judgment on the statement by the filmmaker, E said to me, in a loud voice, "Vietnam is free, motherfucker!" An insult that called for an equally insulting response but do keep in mind that E was nicknamed for one of the most notorious mass murderers in American history. I was not eager to escalate tensions, for the sake of my own safety and that of the other viewers in the room. I chose to let it go.

A day or two later, one of my suitemates named Jeff quietly told me that he agreed with my sentiment. It was nice to know I had an ally, even though Jeff had remained silent at the time of the original exchange, and I could have used the support.

I have since rethought my Vietnam Moment and come to slightly different conclusions. I now believe that the observation that "Vietnam is free" probably referred as much to the American withdrawal as it did the political life of the nation: An ambiguous statement, but not solely a case of left-wing naiveté. It was well past time for the American military to end the madness.

And then, in the fall of 2017, I watched over the course of one week all 10 episodes of the Ken Burns PBS documentary on the war in Vietnam. It had been 42 years since the chaotic exit from Saigon. Vietnam was now an ally of the United States, and many thousands of Vietnamese had settled in the United States since 1975, absorbed into a society that has variously regarded them with admiration, suspicion, and contempt. Americans born in the 1970s, 1980s, and 1990s had experienced their own wars, pushing Vietnam into the background.

But more than four decades after the end of hostilities, I was unexpectedly moved hearing the stories of what the North Vietnamese and Viet Cong endured from 1954 to 1975. My adolescent beliefs, heavily influenced by the constant presence of liberal academics, had only taken into account the political immorality of the American involvement: An undeclared war, we had no business being there, the Domino Theory was absurd. I had never considered the human and material consequences of U.S. actions, especially the incessant bombing.

I still think it was misleading to claim at the 1975 Academy Awards that Vietnam "is free." And I will never accept E calling me "motherfucker." But I was wrong, too. Vietnam was finally done with the American War, as it's called over there. That point needed to be recognized.

*   *   *

For financial reasons, I transferred from Brandeis to Pitzer College in my hometown of Claremont following my freshman year. A week before I left Waltham, my suitemates threw a year-end party, which included a brief ceremony in my honor witnessed by dozens of drunk and stoned attendees. In the early morning hours, I was presented with a robin's egg blue t-shirt that said in red letters "Hassenfeld Hummers." "Hassenfeld" was the name of the dorm we shared. "Hummers" was a descriptive term for women who hum while in the process of giving blow jobs, supposedly enhancing the experience. One of the guys in the suite shared this information with the rest of us, and the idea caught on. When it comes to sex, impressionable, mostly inexperienced young men are willing to believe almost anything.

I packed the t-shirt with the rest of my clothes and flew to Southern California at the end of the semester, late May 1975. I spent the summer doing several jobs — painting dorm rooms, painting houses, stamping and bundling newspapers, and, at the end, working in retail at Winchell's Donuts, which lasted into the summer of 1976. The store was down the street from a club that featured local groups who aspired to be Deep Purple or Led Zeppelin. One night a patron of the club walked in and, giggling, requested a "cocaine donut." It took me a few moments to realize he meant plain cake with powdered sugar on top.

CHAPTER 15

"When We Get Married"

The Dreamlovers, 1961

In college, I hid my love for Doo Wop from all but my closest friends, although even they thought it was strange. When I transferred to Pitzer College, in the fall of 1975, I would only listen to slow ballads from the rock and roll era when no one else was present in my dorm room. I couldn't let cool druggies who worshipped Little Feat, Pink Floyd, and, of course, the Grateful Dead know that I preferred "When We Get Married" by the Dreamlovers, "Teardrops" by Lee Andrews and the Hearts, or "My True Story" by the Jive Five.

I only came out, sort of, in the second semester of my senior year, when it didn't make a difference, since I was a lame duck anyway. My friend Dave and I performed "Baby Talk" by Jan and Dean — which was actually surf Doo Wop — and Dion's "Lonely Teenager" at the all-college talent show. We both sang, and I played acoustic guitar. The two of us improvised some goofy stage antics and in between songs asked a few trivia questions, relating to the era. The crowd laughed during the performance and applauded vigorously after it ended. A few coeds visited my dorm room later to tell me how much they enjoyed the performance. That night remains one of the greatest in my life.

According to the standard definition, I'm not a romantic person. I have rarely given girlfriends candy or flowers, and I have a mixed record on Valentine's Day cards, which I've been told many times is an unforgivable sin. But in the presence of Doo Wop music, I turn into a dreamboat. On several occasions—parties and one-on-one—I have slow danced with girlfriends, and girls who are friends, to ballads from the late 50s and early 60s. I would put on a record, beckon the woman closer, and like the perfect gentleman take the lead. I never had dance lessons, but I was very careful to synchronize my movements with those of my partner — stumbling and giggling would have instantly killed the mood. I was determined to recreate in my own way that magic moment at the high school hop when the lights dim and the band plays a slow number—just like it happens in the movies.

I did receive criticism on occasion for choosing songs that told a sad story of love lost or love unreciprocated, which was not exactly the message my partner wished to receive. A valid point, but as I explained, what mattered most were the harmonies and melody, lyrics not so much.

Slow dancing to the oldies conferred another benefit, apart from the warmth of intimacy. It was my own way of rejecting ultra-cool, antiromantic romanticism, very popular in the late 70s and 80s. That style seemed to me pretentious and trite, an obvious art school mockery of pop culture. I danced cheek-to-cheek with several staunch feminists, the two of us stepping lightly across the brown-carpeted living room of my small North Hollywood apartment in the early 80s. I would ask my date if she wanted to hear some quiet music, without specifying what type. In an era of head-banging heavy metal and full-throttle punk, she would be pleasantly surprised by the request, and usually answer with something along the lines of "Yes, of course." I would walk over to the cassette player, in which I had already cued a 30-minute tape of 50s ballads, and with a flourish push the play button.

My apartment would instantly be filled with melodic disquisitions on the unpredictable nature of young love, the vocalists accompanied by session musicians capable of stunningly beautiful riffs on bass, guitar, or piano. I would stand in the middle of the room and motion the young lady to rise from the couch. If this was our first time, she would move with a bit of hesitation, not entirely sure what I had in mind. I welcomed her uncertainty; it probably indicated that she had not done this with other guys, or at all. I wanted to believe that I had the retro slow dance market all to myself.

When the music started, we behaved like lovebirds at the time of the New Frontier: holding each other tight, whispered conversations, swooning to the gorgeous harmonies. Doo Wop was the food of love.

CHAPTER 16

"Always and Forever"

Heatwave, 1977

By the middle 1970s, soul ballads, the successor to Doo Wop, had become almost nonexistent. Marvin Gaye's "Let's Get it On" from 1973 was a gorgeous exception, an exquisite marriage of love and sex, Motown channeling high-end French cinema. One of the only ballads I know where you can sing along with the melodic guitar lines, provided in this case by Ray Parker, Jr.

I was never a fan of Blue Magic, the Manhattans, or the Stylistics, whose singles seemed to me manipulative and corny, readymade for parody. (As I recall, *The Gong Show* took them up on the unsolicited offer, and more than once.) I kind of liked the Chi-Lites — the use of a mournful harmonica on "Oh, Girl" was innovative — but not enough to buy their records. To fill in the gap, I turned to pop ballads of the day, a few of which were excellent, such as the Hollies' "He Ain't Heavy, He's My Brother," and "Precious and Few," a wholesome song recorded by a group with a blue movie moniker, Climax. Pete Wingfield's "Eighteen with a Bullet" (1975) captured the sound, but the song was intended as a joke, lyrics taken from music industry lingo.

I had reluctantly adjusted to life without new and soulful slow dance numbers when I heard a song come over the radio in the spring of 1978 that sounded to me like a forgotten treasure from 10, 12 years earlier. The arrangement, vocals, and words were true to the genre, which was the first and most important test. When you crave a dying art form, you have to be on guard for those who would exploit your feelings and provide cynical copies of the Real Thing. I also appreciated that the song was in a key that I could duplicate without much effort. I wasn't much of a vocalist, but I had a decent ear, and could usually sing along without causing too much sonic discomfort to myself or the people around me.

The song was called "Always and Forever," a title so smart that I was sure it must have been "borrowed" from one that had been released before the rock era, although I never found proof of that. It was recorded by a group called Heatwave on the Epic label, which provided another connection. My girlfriend at the time really liked an earlier single by the same group called "Boogie Nights," a bass-heavy disco number that could not have been more different from "Always and Forever." I was polite and circumspect about "Boogie Nights," but in truth I thought the song was rather silly, beginning with the title. I knew nothing about Heatwave, but on the basis of my own musical arrogance, I figured they were destined for a quick exit, like so many other disco-influenced acts. When I discovered the translucent "Always and Forever" was by the same group, I ran from my dorm room to my girlfriend's dorm room — a distance of about 300 yards — to deliver the good news. We hugged, and she said, "I told you so," or words to that effect.

The song cast a retro, romantic sheen over a college experience that was more in line with the changing sexual mores of the late 1970s. It isn't always clean or neat, but you can have it both ways, thereabouts.

*   *   *

In my senior year, 1977–1978, I lived in a suite at Pitzer that was aligned with my cultural values. Less acid, more beer, less ethereal folk, more funk. Sartorial choices that didn't suggest life was a nonstop Grateful Dead concert. Though still socially awkward, I felt much more at ease in this environment, even ventured outside my single room to join impromptu gatherings.

Plus, those parties I mentioned earlier, the women dressed in stylish dresses, the men in slacks and sport coats, like frat boys and sorority girls, but without the hazing, binge drinking, and asinine politics. The preparation was as much fun as the event. A few of us would gather in one room and make party tapes, each picking a song, in order, until we had compiled three hours of recorded music. A notably eclectic mix, including 60s and 70s rock, Motown, soul ballads, funk, Elvis and Little Richard, the Ramones, Springsteen, Patti Smith, and disco. On the night of the party, the music committee would act like proud parents, watching the masses dance to our selections.

By this point, I had acquired a new girlfriend, who lived down the hall. My first girlfriend and I had broken up the summer after my sophomore year. She had started to find me boring and wanted to see other guys.

I was devastated. For the next several weeks I turned apocalyptic, telling those close to me that I would never have another girlfriend, because no female would ever want me as her boyfriend. Although I was living in an era of heightened sexual activity, I proclaimed that I would most likely remain celibate for the rest of my life, not by choice. I also entertained this odd idea—which had no actuarial or spiritual basis—that losing my virginity was much easier to achieve than having sex with a second person, like writing a second novel is supposedly much more difficult than writing the first.

It took eight or nine months before I made it to #2. Her name was Kathy, and we were coworkers in the college library. It was a spring/summer romance that had a pre-arranged end date; she was a senior who would be headed off to graduate school in economics in late August. Kathy was adorable, blonde, and witty. I thought of her as a charming, vivacious English woman whose personality had miraculously formed in the suburbs of Southern California. We parted on great terms, exchanged a few letters, and continued with our lives.

I started going out with my Pitzer girlfriend in November. Soon we were sleeping together exclusively, in a committed relationship, all very tidy and adult. This was my first and as it turned out my only on-campus romance (I was living at home when I was involved with Kathy.) The arrangement had the distinct advantages of access and proximity. We each had our own dorm rooms, which were located a couple of hundred yards apart, the distance between the women's section and the men's section. There were no checkpoints or impossible-to-navigate barriers separating the two. This was what students wanted, around the country, and college administrators were amenable, as college administrators tend to be, especially at expensive private institutions.

At Pitzer, I finally came in direct contact with the Sexual Revolution, meeting women who were actually on the front lines. Like all revolutionaries, they had their hallowed texts; Erica Jong's *Fear of Flying* and Sara Davidson's *Loose Change*, novels based at least in part on real experiences and real women who made a convincing case The Vagina can be as active as The Penis, sometimes more so. In the pages of these works of "fiction," social constraints and sexist double standards were no match for unquenchable desire, fearlessness, and cunning.

My scant knowledge of promiscuity came from men's magazines, mainly *Playboy*. Yet, I didn't assume that Hef was actually having sex with most of these women, only that they were part of his seemingly unlimited pool of talent. In high school, one from time to time heard degrading comments about some girl who sleeps around, behaves like a whore or slut. But my virginal self had no way of translating such scurrilous and sexist gossip into informed speculation. I was not the ideal audience for these rumors, obviously.

At Pitzer, I heard stories from reliable sources of women who had slept with 10 or 20 men or more. I also heard stories of women who in real life had enacted the "Zipless Fuck," made famous in *Fear of Flying*. While I was watching TV on a Friday night or listening to a ball game on a Saturday night, these ladies were in hot pursuit of sensual pleasures and making social history at the same time, compiling numbers that far exceeded previous generations of American women. They were enjoying sex for its own sake, which was supposedly not a female proclivity, at least among the white middle class.

At the time, my senior year at Pitzer, I had slept with four women. Not the stats of a stud, but a decent record for a guy with abysmal social skills. That's what I thought, anyway. But after hearing about what else was going on out there — especially with women — I felt completely inadequate, a walking embarrassment. I became depressed and moody, acting like a deprived child, and yet I also couldn't handle the truth. I had been robbed of my male entitlement and sense of superiority, which as any guy will tell you, is a terrible blow to the psyche.

I will say one thing in my favor. During this bleak period, I didn't question even privately why a woman would want to sleep with numerous partners. Although I was losing the game, and felt lousy about that, I recognized no gender distinction in the pursuit of carnal delights. In that sense, I was a liberated man.

Still, it took me several years to reconcile myself to the reality that thousands of American females were reaping the benefits of the New Morality, far beyond my meager attempts to join in. After graduating from Pitzer, I continued to brood over my fate. I would read articles written by women celebrating their carnal escapades, which would leave me feeling both fascinated and profoundly morose. By this point, gay men had started to publish their own sex-heavy confessionals, with partners numbering in the hundreds or thousands. The authors were acting on their desires in a manner and to a degree I couldn't imagine. I felt like a guy who failed to invest in a winning stock, watching everyone else get rich.

And then, in the early 1980s, I decided to sit back, relax, and enjoy it. I transformed myself into a true blue American pragmatist regarding the changing sexual habits of the American female. What was the alternative? Continuing to be the poor, pathetic guy alone in the corner, feeling glum that he wasn't a teenager during the era when boy/girl relations resembled the lyrics of a Tab Hunter song? Starting in college, and continuing unabated as I entered the workforce, I found myself in the presence of women who had had various sexual experiences, and if asked by a person they could trust were happy to share details. At that time, 1980–1982, I was embarking on a career as a journalist, and honing my interviewing skills, which would serve me well in life and work. I gradually learned to listen and ask pertinent follow-up questions. My job depended on it.

Around 1983–1984, I did a complete flip-flop, and decided that women with busy sex lives were the more desirable, all other things being relatively equal. Exhibiting the zeal of the newly converted, I vigorously pursued my sisters in the Sexual Revolution.

I drew the mature, worldly conclusion—or so I thought—that women who had lots of sex must really love sex. I refused to entertain other explanations, some of them flat-out sexist. I was profoundly skeptical of the notion propagated by therapists—many of them women—that female promiscuity was motivated by some deep, psychological yearning, such as getting back at mom or finding a substitute for dad. Such theories, offered under the general heading of self-help, also provided a kind of psychological comfort for those who didn't go wild, reassurance that their way was best. At the same time, however, male promiscuity was not commonly regarded as errant behavior, but something natural to the species. Why was it different for women? Was the pleasure principle only for guys? Seeing these women, meeting these women, cured me of the accursed Male Double Standard.

Such was my philosophy during my impressionable 20s. In my wise 30s, I stopped making value judgments around sexual histories. Not stopped, exactly, but put it in proper perspective, one factor among many, including how the other person felt about "Always and Forever."

CHAPTER 17

"Eve of Destruction"

Barry McGuire, 1965/The Dickies, 1978

When I really liked a particular 45, I would study the label to learn the names of the people responsible for making me this happy: composer—sole or with others—producer, in some cases the arranger as well. My gratitude to these musical geniuses was not unlike what I felt for a favorite sports team the year it won a championship. It was if the various contributors had generously assembled and recorded the song for the express purpose of bringing me joy. Like the great works of art, these pop music miracles were essential to life, my life. Without them, there would be little sense in carrying on.

In later years, long after the singles had been released, I had telephone interviews with a few of these wonderful people, whose names I had memorized for eternity. Along with my close friend, David Reyes, I was one of the producers of a three-volume compilation for Rhino Records entitled *Brown-Eyed Soul*. The collection, which came out in

1997, included songs that had either been massively popular with the Latino community of Southern California or featured a sound that resonated with that audience. David and I had a splendid time choosing the music for the compilation; personal favorites along with fantastic records that absolutely had to make the cut, such as "The Town I Live In" by Thee Midniters, "Together" by Tierra, and "Me and You" by Brenton Wood. It felt as if we were bringing joy to people, contributing to pop music history, and throwing a huge party—all in one.

Along with serving on the selection committee, I had the job of writing the liner notes accompanying each song. Rather than just offer a glowing review, my goal was whenever possible to speak to the creator or creators behind the record, add their anecdotes or reflections. Finding them involved in many cases a bit of detective work, which I enjoyed nearly as much as the interviews themselves. I would be required to track down the person, sometimes more than one, who would lead me to The Person. It was even better when the song in question was obscure, and there was no immediate, obvious path that led to the producer and/or composer.

Two of the selections that beautifully represented the sound we wanted to capture were "Baby, Is There Something on Your Mind" by McKinley Travis that came out in the summer of 1970, and "Let's Get Together Again" by Carol Hughes, released in the summer of 1968. Each received minimal airplay and fell far short of the *Billboard* Top 100 pop charts.

I was 13 years old in a car with my parents heading north on the 605 Freeway in Southeast Los Angeles County, when I first heard "Baby, Is There Something on Your Mind" on my favorite station at the time, KHJ-AM. It was a soul opera in miniature, grand entrance of strings and spoken words followed by the pleadings of a man trying to find a happy medium with his jealous wife/girlfriend. I was hooked even before the second crescendo, when the instruments cede the stage to the singer, who proceeds to define what it means to be a "good, good woman" in the company of "a good, good man." In those days, I was gawky and self-conscious, yet I started interpreting the song like James Brown at the Apollo in front of my highly amused parents.

Whenever I had a crush on a new single, I would go the next day to one of several local record stores and add it to my collection. With this song, however, I had to wait almost a week. For whatever reason, "Baby, Is There Something on Your Mind" was only getting played on KHJ. A number of the stores I frequented were not carrying the record and had no plans to do so. I finally located a copy at an establishment called Discount Records, which in the case of 45s, did not live up to its name. Still, I was now in possession of this magnificent specimen of soul.

After a few weeks, I started to take "Baby" for granted and moved on to other singles, a familiar pattern with me. My passion for the song never wavered, but I might go for weeks or months between hearing it on my modest stereo system. Since "Baby" had bombed on the charts — an unforgivable sin committed by the teens of America in the summer of 1970 — the song was not included in any station's playlist for oldies weekends. The only way for me to hear the record was if I played it myself.

In 1996, when Rhino approved the concept for "Brown-Eyed Soul," I had an opportunity to properly thank "Baby, Is There Something on Your Mind" for the joy it brought into my life. David Reyes had a phenomenal collection of Doo Wop and soul singles, and it didn't surprise me that he also possessed a copy of "Baby." We agreed to include it on the anthology, another prime example of the sound that captivated East Los Angeles.

I quickly determined that within my allotted time it would be too difficult to track down McKinley Travis, but Bobby Sanders, the composer and producer of the song, was accessible. When I first bought the record, I noted his name on the label, part of the creative team behind this work of soul genius. I spoke to Bobby on a weekday afternoon, door closed to my day job office. Before we formally began the interview, I told him how much his record had meant to me, a socially awkward white eighth-grader from the suburbs. To this day, I would like to think that I was the first and last of my kind to pay homage to Bobby for giving the world "Baby." He expressed gratitude for the compliment and added that he was pleased by my response to the song all those years ago. I told him I still loved it, nearly three decades later, which pleased him even more.

The entire conversation lasted maybe 15 minutes. I got the basic story and wrote it up for the liner notes. But I will always be thrilled that I had the chance to speak to Bobby Sanders, composer and producer of one of the greatest if unheralded ballads in the history of soul music.

*   *   *

"Let's Get Together Again" was based on a theme more common to the Southern California stable of white pop records: What happens to a boy/girl couple after high school ends, and things change? The singer is hoping to rekindle the feeling, and the hopeful tone of the record implies that she just might succeed. I certainly bought the premise, in large part because I had a high school romance that was negatively affected by the realities of life after graduation. (We lasted another two years.)

In its production and, especially, the lead vocals, "Let's Get Together Again" strongly resembled the early 60s singles recorded by Mary Wells prior to "My Guy." I enjoyed those records much more than "My Guy," which sounded comparatively calculated and slick. Unlike "Baby, Is There Something on Your Mind," I first heard "Let's Get Together Again" two decades after its initial release. I was not in the moment, as they say, having graduated from high school 15–20 years earlier. Yet, I could easily imagine similar feelings, not for reasons of nostalgia, but because I recognized that moving on from high school provides an emotional preview of the significant changes that occur throughout our lives.

I remember walking through the snow at Brandeis with a fellow freshman named Jay, who suddenly stopped and asked: "Man, do you know how old we are?" "Do you know?" I had not considered age 18 old, just older. Yet, I understood his point. The onset of adult responsibilities meant we were no longer technically young. We now had far more in common with people who were 30 than people who were 12. Though we were only in the first quarter of our lives — according to the data — Jay and I and millions of others in the Class of 1974 had already gone through high school, a seminal event, comparable to losing one's virginity and getting that first full-time job, which typically occur within that same timeframe. Many young men and young women hated high school, for educational and social reasons, and were only too glad to have it over. I occasionally felt that way myself, although in the end, the good outweighed the bad.

I was receptive to "Let's Get Together Again," because it sounded legitimate, devoid of the cheap sentiment with which a Top 40 tune would handle the same theme. I was also intrigued that an idea from white pop culture had been appropriated by a Black singer, in direct contrast to the usual pattern. I first heard the song from David Reyes, and then occasionally on KRLA, which at that time was programming oldies geared to the Latino audience. David and I agreed without hesitation to add the song to the Rhino collection.

I read a name on the label—Doug Cox, writer and producer — and eventually traced him to Las Vegas, where I believe he worked as a motivational trainer. As with Bobby Sanders, I was in awe of Doug Cox, who had created on vinyl ~2:20 minutes of sublime beauty that will last forever. Their stories were different, however. Doug was a white guy who had this idea for taking the typical post-high school reunion song and giving it a soul twist. He found a talented local singer, Carol Hughes, and conveyed a mood with the lyrics and production that made it seem as if this particular subgenre was always meant for a Black woman performer. The best song of its kind that I have ever heard, no other comes close.

After hanging up with Doug, I had that same blissful, privileged sensation that followed my brief interview with Bobby. Once again, I had found the person behind a little known single that covered me with chills and shivers, even as a man.

*   *   *

In the early summer of 2014, I interviewed the songwriter P.F. (Phil) Sloan over lunch at the same Santa Monica deli from where I had interviewed Peter Tork 16 years earlier. I was writing a column about pop music of the 1960s and 1970s for a website that covered the arts in Southern California. I timed my articles, which typically ran between 1500 and 2000 words, to the release of a new boxed set or book. Sloan arrived at our meeting in the company of his prose collaborator, S.E. (Steve) Feinberg. Phil and Steve had written the recently published *What's Exactly the Matter With Me? Memoirs of a Life in Music.* The book recounted Sloan's story from his days as 1950s kid in love with Elvis and rock and roll to the present, having achieved emotional equilibrium after experiencing the highest of highs and the lowest of lows.

I had been curious about Sloan for many years. His name kept appearing on some of my favorite singles from the 1960s — "Let Me Be," "You Baby (Nobody but You)," "Secret Agent Man," and "Eve of Destruction" — but each of them had been hits for other people. I had never even seen a photo of the guy, as opposed to the artists who had benefitted from his creative talents. No idea if he was tall or short, stocky or thin, crazed or unassuming — a bona fide rock and roll mystery. Doing the basic math, I figured he was in his late 60s, but that was the extent of my knowledge.

When I arrived at the deli, I immediately started looking for males who fit the Sloan demographic. There were a number of candidates, but I was wary of approaching them. Older men are not always the kindest people on the planet. Some of them can be genuine assholes.

If I had known ahead of time that Feinberg would be coming to lunch as well, it would have made my search much easier, eliminating immediately the solo diners as possibilities. About 10 minutes after I got to the place, I heard two men engaged in an intense conversation about the war in Iraq and America's options in the Middle East. On the basis of "Eve of Destruction" (#1, 1965, recorded by Barry McGuire), I had long ago identified Sloan as a political person. I took a chance that one of these discussants was the guy I was supposed to interview. I guessed right.

For the next 90 minutes, Phil mixed the personal with the musical, talked about his life as a fan and a contributor, especially the feverish few days in 1965 when he wrote a series of memorable songs, including "Eve of Destruction," one of my favorite singles from a fertile period in rock and roll. I came to the record several years after its release, when most of the events or phenomena that it name-checks were no longer in the forefront of the American agenda. Yet, for me, a fervent history buff, the immediate topicality of the lyrics was irrelevant. As with the liner notes to *December's Children*, the song provided me the irresistible opportunity to participate in the drama of the mid-1960s, which I was too young to notice the first time. In fact, I have a weakness for lyrics taken from the pages of history, such as "American Pie" or the much less popular "Post-World War II Blues" by Al Stewart. Part of this was showing off, demonstrating to friends that I knew the back stories to the events noted in these records. But I also felt that these songs were written especially for me, someone who got as excited talking about *Rubber Soul* as I did discussing the battle of Dien Bien Phu.

Phil was patient and gracious, sharing the details of his own story—a mind-blowing spate of creativity, encounters with the gods of rock and roll in Los Angeles and London, dealings with duplicitous industry types, the end of his hit-making days, years of wandering, seeking answers and inner peace, and, finally, a triumphant re-emergence, through the book and live performances. Near the end of our time together, I mentioned to Phil and Steve that in a few hours I would be attending the first reading of a musical I had written based on a true rock and roll story — an East LA vocal group called Cannibal and the Headhunters opening for the Beatles at the Hollywood Bowl—taken from the same year that "Eve of Destruction" was released. The two of them generously asked questions about how and where I discovered the story, my writing process, and whether I had a plan in mind for the musical. I was both flattered and touched that P.F. Sloan of all people would show such interest in my work, which at that point was nothing more than words on a page.

I remained in periodic contact with Steve and Phil over the next several months. I booked Phil as a guest on a local Los Angeles television show I created and hosted called *Rock and Roll Stories* and attended two of his musical performances plus a book signing. Steve was a critical factor in the evolution of the musical from concept to reality.

In the fall of 2015, Phil died from a typically aggressive and swift form of pancreatic cancer. I feel lucky to have known Mr. Sloan, and I regret that I never told him the story of how I stumbled upon an amped-up cover version of his masterpiece, more than a decade after it entered the charts.

     *   *   *

After graduating from Pitzer College in May 1978, I decided to take a year away from formal education. When I made the decision, which wasn't difficult after 16 consecutive years of schooling, I had no plan. I never before held a full-time job, except during the summer, and now I would need to find one. But where, and what?

I was no closer to answering those questions in late July than I was on the bleary morning after graduation. Time was running out.

During an extended lunch break from our furniture delivery job, my coworker and close friend, Joel, and I visited a Tower Records that had recently opened in the city of West Covina, located about halfway between Claremont and downtown Los Angeles. As the two of us browsed, in different sections, I started talking to a friendly clerk who was stylishly dressed in black leather pants and an untucked white blouse. She turned out to be the person responsible for maintaining the store's substantial punk rock section.

With slight embarrassment, I told her I remained partial to 60s rock, I just couldn't help myself. She reassured me there was no need to apologize, she loved that music as well, but punk was new, punk was thrilling, and punk was essential. I asked this young woman what she meant by that, and she told me to look around the store. With ill-disguised contempt, she pointed out the big-haired girls and long-haired boys purchasing albums by Boston, Journey, Kansas, and Queen. Having grown up in a sophisticated college town, where young people tried to outdo themselves with their obscure musical obsessions, I was blissfully ignorant of the predominant tastes of middle-class American record buyers. But in this culturally flat environment it made sense that punk, with its rank anticommercialism and Embrace of the Ugly, would serve as a seductive alternative for certain disaffected, intelligent young people who fervently resisted local norms. That division was not so stark in Claremont.

After I expressed mild skepticism about punk's sonic appeal, my hostess took me into the store's empty classical music room, which was closed off from the main store, and promptly disappeared. A minute later she returned carrying an EP featuring "Eve of Destruction," but not the familiar version performed by Barry McGuire. This rendition was attributed to a contemporary group called the Dickies. At that time, I vaguely recalled the original single, with its references to contemporary political events, including Selma, Alabama, the People's Republic of China (we referred to it then as Red China), and space exploration. I hadn't heard it for years.

The clerk had cleverly chosen to meet me halfway, punk interprets the 60s. She slowly removed the sleeve from the record, which was covered in creamy white vinyl, an industry gimmick at that time. Wearing a sly smile, she placed it on the turntable. Within seconds I was hearing a new kind of rock and roll insanity, chords and lyrics engaged in a blistering, frantic competition to the finish line. As far as I could tell, none of the political references had been changed, providing a humorous juxtaposition of an ultra-modern sound with retro lyrics.

When the song was over, in less than two minutes, I attempted to make sense of what I had heard. Was this maniacal version supposed to be a tribute, a joke, a parody, a death knell for Sunset Strip folk rock, all of the above? I desperately needed context.

Still, to ask such questions was to fall into a familiar trap, the old fogey (all of 21, in my case) trying to discern what the "kids" intended. Rather than seeking answers, engaging in a discussion, I retreated to that old familiar standby and declared this version "interesting." I accompanied that bland word with a puzzled look, as if I were in the process of placing the Dickies' song on the rock continuum.

The clerk seemed pleased by my apparent open-mindedness. I got the impression that she had tried this out on other hopeless 60s addicts, who had responded with the predictable agonized wails. But I had at least shown a modicum of respect.

Some 30 years later, I played the Dickies' version of "Eve of Destruction" during a minilecture on Southern California rock that I gave to a group of high school students, including my eldest son, Zach. When the song had finished, one of the girls in attendance proclaimed it "awesome." Who was I to disagree?

CHAPTER 18

"We Belong Together"

Robert and Johnny, 1958

I worked at the Tower Records in West Covina from 1978 to 1981, thanks in part to the friendly scion of the punk rock section. She encouraged me to take the music history test for prospective employees, and I scored in the 90th percentile.

For in-store entertainment and their own sonic pleasure, staff was allowed to play albums from the massive collection. The LPs were then resealed on a machine in the upstairs lounge and returned to the floor, sold as new product. I was once challenged by a friend who said the practice amounted to fraud. I responded if that was the case, every department store in the country committed the same offense, selling articles of clothing that had been tried on by one or more people of varying sizes, shapes, and hygiene practices. Irrelevant, declared my friend, who had hoped rock and roll would be better than this.

A couple of months into my tenure, I felt comfortable enough with my coworkers to choose a Doo Wop album for my selection, an incongruous addition to a list overloaded with punk, disco, Rush, and Cheap Trick. Colleagues may have not been impressed, but a sizeable number of customers loved that music, generation after generation. Tower was located near several cities with a majority Latino population, including Azusa, Baldwin Park, and El Monte. When I started working at the store, I was already aware that the Latino community had a long-standing passion for romantic ballads, most of them recorded by Black artists. Southern California in the 1970s had two major AM radio stations that primarily programmed this genre of music, KRLA and XTRA, which was based in Baja, California, and had a powerhouse signal that penetrated much of the western United States. During the evening hours, KRLA took listener requests over the air. Even an Anglo who was rather ignorant of Mexican-American culture at the time—I'm referring to myself—could determine after a few days of listening to KRLA that the vast majority of requests came from areas with a large Latino population. It was because of the size of that audience that fans like me heard more classic ballads over the air than we had any right to expect in the late 1970s.

One of the songs on the collection, "We Belong Together" by an African-American, New York duo called Robert and Johnny remained a major hit with Latino audiences 20 and 30 years after its release in 1958. It was covered by Ritchie Valens a few months before his death in a plane crash at the age of 17 and by Los Lobos in the late 1980s. "We Belong Together" combines a confident prediction of love's inevitability with tender harmonies, as if the narrator is being careful not to appear brash or self-assured. The object of his affection and desire is never identified or described. She is simply the other half of the "We" in the title. The vocals are augmented by a series of well-placed guitar notes, a common occurrence on Doo Wop singles.

My selection of "We Belong Together" garnered favorable attention from one Tower employee. His name was David Reyes and he had started working at the store roughly the same time as I did. His hair extended halfway down his back and he usually chose modern jazz or contemporary classical for his in-store album choices. I did not assume that he was also a devotee of Doo Wop.

Apparently David thought the same thing about me: He didn't expect a Caucasian who attended a private college to like romantic ballads from the 1950s and early 1960s. I offered a radical contrast to my demographic, which preferred rock that was experimental, smart, and self-aware. In my presence, David would tell friends of mine that he was pleasantly surprised by my passion for "We Belong Together" and the like. My friends had the good manners to smile and nod, but I don't think they were all that impressed.

David and I started to spend time together, inside and outside Tower, drawn to each other by one song, and then many, plus sports and the arts. We would seek out record shops that stocked 45s from the past, attend Lakers and Rams games, and visit hip or esoteric bookstores. In those early days, before I became spoiled, I regarded our friendship as a kind of miracle. I had never guessed that I would meet someone who knew much more than I did about R&B ballads from 1955–1965. Until I connected with

David, there was no one with whom I could discuss these songs without having to first explain why I liked them so much in the first place. I have always believed that intelligent conversations about works of art or pop culture can be as stimulating as the thing itself, sometimes more so. I have spent more hours than I could possibly count talking and arguing about films, plays, books, and rock and roll. Thanks to David, I added rhythm and blues and soul to the list.

David had an unusually eclectic background in music, beyond Doo Wop. He was a saxophonist who played in several R&B groups that performed in and around his hometown of Pomona, which happened to be right next to my hometown of Claremont. He was also a composer of modern classical music, who counted among his idols Morton Gould, John Cage, and Karlheinz Stockhausen. His vast collection of singles and LPs ranged from the dreamily accessible to the difficult and obtuse. I have always been attracted to the people with unpredictable tastes, who deviate from the pattern that is supposedly implied by their gender, ethnicity, race, age, or appearance. I yearn for the day when a young Black, Brown, or white person pulls up next to me at a stoplight with his car stereo system blasting Beethoven or Brahms. It hasn't happened yet, but I remain hopeful.

A couple of years into our friendship, David and I became collaborators, partners in search of projects. We could not have imagined at the time that we would spend much of the next three decades telling the story of Chicano rock and roll through one form or another.

      *   *   *

There are several advantages to having a professor for a parent: sabbaticals, lively dinner parties, which can provide an intellectual spark, even when one is in elementary school, a wide range of interesting books in the house, available for reading at any time, and in my case, tickets to University of California at Berkeley basketball and football games in 1967 and 1968. During my junior year of college, I discovered another advantage, of sorts. My professor father had inside knowledge of job prospects in academia. At the end of the 1970s, they weren't promising, to put it mildly.

There were too many people with doctoral degrees chasing too few positions, especially in the humanities. My dad offered a stark example from his own employer, Harvey Mudd College. The school had an opening for a tenure track English professor; 435 candidates applied. He didn't indicate how many of these applicants were "serious," and I didn't think to ask, but it really didn't matter. I was fairly confident of my intellectual abilities, but I also knew that among 435 candidates, I would be lucky to finish at the bottom of the Top 100. I was too much the inherent pessimist to believe that in six years, or however long it took me to get a Ph.D., the situation would have improved even a little. Dissuaded by the realities of the job market, I opted not to pursue an advanced degree in history, which had been my vague goal since junior high.

In an unsystematic way, I cast about for alternatives. I thought about law school — l enjoyed a good argument, had a quick mind — but I was turned off by the realization that after getting my law degree I would have to become a lawyer. I thought briefly about business school, but I was lousy with numbers, and making money didn't much matter to me.

After weeks of further deliberations, I found the answer—journalism school. I loved to read newspapers, and that plus my background in history was, or so I presumed at the time, a necessary prerequisite to working as a reporter. There was one minor drawback to my new pursuit: I had written only a few articles for the college paper and had no real understanding of how to put together a story. Many applicants would have already compiled a portfolio of impressive bylines, placing me at a competitive disadvantage. Still, I was confident that my otherwise solid background would more than compensate for my deficiencies. This assumption, grounded more in hope than reality, turned out to be correct.

In the fall of 1979, I enrolled in a master's program in journalism at USC. But before starting my classes, I had to set aside a lifelong antipathy toward the institution. I had been heavily influenced by two former UC Berkeley graduate students — my own mother and father — who despised USC and everything it represented. They regarded the school as a font of noxious conservatism, populated in the main by bullies, braggarts, and the entitled sons and daughters of privilege. My parents formed these opinions in the late 1940s, and nothing that had happened between then and the end of the 1970s had caused them to change their minds. In fact, USC had recently served as a farm team for the Watergate scandal, the alma mater of a disproportionate number of liars and dirty tricksters, including the smarmy Donald Segretti. When the USC connection to Nixon's men and Watergate became known, my parents and their liberal friends were not the least bit surprised.

Mostly because of mom and dad, I became virulently anti-Trojan, especially toward the football team, which to me represented the worst of the worst. Every time the team made a good play, the band would perform this riff that sounded like the march of a mighty imperial army into a small, overmatched nation. Those relatively few notes embodied the overweening sense of pride and unapologetic arrogance that I associated with USC.

I openly rooted against the football team in the late 1960s and early 1970s, when the Trojans had one of the greatest periods in their history. The team's tremendous success only made me hate them more of course. It was unbearable to think of all those blond frat boys and sorority girls having their gridiron fantasies fulfilled.

My parents were more amused than disappointed by my decision to apply to, and attend, USC. They thought journalism school was a good idea, but they also knew that my choices were limited, due to my lack of experience in the field and less-than-distinguished academic record. Plus, I would be an entering graduate student, which in theory should limit my exposure to the dark side of USC, otherwise known as undergraduates. I stood a good chance of receiving my MA degree without being politically tainted.

As it happened, I took classes taught by highly opinionated left-wing professors. All that worry was for nothing. A few months after graduating at USC, I was hired as a part-time reporter for the *San Gabriel Valley Tribune*. It took three months and several stories before I showed my editors that I might have the stuff to become an actual journalist. By that point I had become painfully aware that they were rewriting my ledes more times than what was considered acceptable, even for a mere part-timer. After submitting an article, I would discreetly watch from across the newsroom, studying the editor's face for evidence of disappointment or exasperation. I was worried and even at times paranoid, but not entirely without reason. Newspaper editors are not known for their unlimited patience.

I began to think seriously that the *Tribune* would let me go. What saved me, if in fact I needed to be saved, was a story I covered early one morning at the Los Angeles County Fair in Pomona. A group of experts had gathered to judge the various wines that would be entered into competition. I was and am a beer person and know virtually nothing about wine. If forced to choose, I will take white over red, but that's like saying I prefer 7-Up to Coke. In this case, my lack of knowledge was a plus. I came to the story with an open mind, ready to be surprised.

Watching the experts sniff then swish various wines in their mouths, spit out the liquid, and cleanse their palettes with crackers, I had the recurring thought: What an odd way to start the morning. Back in the newsroom I turned that thought into my lead, which read like this; "At 7 a.m., when most people are thinking of orange juice, wine tasters at the LA County Fair found themselves staring at glasses of chardonnay and pinot noir." My editors, delighted and surprised, actually showed the lede to each other, like proud teachers whose faith in their chronically underperforming student had finally been vindicated. Then they called me over to offer praise and congratulations. I had made the cut, barely.

In March 1982, the *Tribune* offered me a full-time position, which I immediately accepted. I was given a beat, the foothill cities of Duarte and Monrovia, each with populations around 25,000. I would be required to regularly cover city council and school board meetings, closely tracking agenda items for anything that had widespread interest or smacked of controversy, preferably both. This posed a challenge for someone who had never paid the slightest attention to municipal politics. I could easily name the last five prime ministers of Great Britain but not the last two mayors of Claremont, still my hometown at that time. Before moving to Los Angeles, I'm not sure I even voted in city elections.

I received my education in municipal government on the job, interviewing city managers, assistant city managers, planning directors, police chiefs, and members of the city council, including the mayor. I pored over the massive agendas issued at least three days prior to the date of the council meeting, by law. I came to enjoy the challenge of discerning which among the 30 or so items would generate the most heat.

One of the continually contentious issues involved the granting of cable television franchises. At that time, the industry was home to numerous providers, not all of which had the technical knowhow or public relations savvy to withstand service delivery crises. The very first Duarte City Council meeting I covered took place on the day after telecast of the Academy Awards and NCAA basketball championship game. Stormy conditions that busy evening had caused hundreds of customers in the foothill portion of the community to lose their picture for all or parts of both events. Numerous sports fans and movie buffs – who in some cases were the same person – attended the meeting, angry at the pathetic cable company and even angrier at the City Council members for approving a deal with it in the first place. Promises from elected officials to do better in the future offered little consolation to residents who had been denied the pleasure of watching two of the showcase events of the year. As was common with small city politics, the public's ire and rage was unrewarded. The company kept the franchise, until much later, when corporate America stepped in. Today, Duarte's service is provided by Spectrum.

Throughout the rest of 1982 and 1983, I covered numerous council meetings in which poorly performing cable franchises were a major topic of discussion. The embattled providers kept sending different emissaries to the meetings, hoping to find the right spokesperson to placate pissed off council members. I interviewed several of these representatives, one of whom had bloodshot eyes and reeked of alcohol. And that was before the meeting even started.

After a few months on the job, I made a successful pitch to become the paper's political reporter, in addition to my regular duties. I got the assignment for the simple reason that I was more interested in politics than the other reporters on staff. I covered Washington from 3,000 miles away and Sacramento from 500 miles away. Much of the job involved telephone interviews and reporting of local speeches delivered before business groups and friendly, partisan organizations. I would scribble notes — many of them undecipherable — on a small, lined pad, and when the event finished, drive quickly to the newsroom, composing much of the article in my head. Not the ideal circumstances to produce brilliant, thoughtful stories, but great training for swift and efficient writing, which is always in demand.

The beat compelled me to pay closer attention to economic legislation, which had never been one of my consuming interests. I studied up on tax-exempt bonds, became familiar with the particular needs of small businesses, charted the progress of various trade bills, and immersed myself in the politics of budget deficits. I can't say that this crash course turned me into an expert, but I know more now than I did before about the American economy, for what it's worth.

Before assuming this beat, I had not set foot inside any political office. No one in my immediate family ever had a reason to call on our House member, Assembly person, or state senator for assistance. I was fundamentally ignorant of how elected officials and more important their staff members interacted with the public. I had, at best, a distant and remote view of the way our system operates, on the ground, information culled mainly from media sources.

I discovered that there are people who actively cultivate access and proximity to an elected official, or elected officials. This broad category encompasses community leaders, heads of non-profit organizations, business advocates, and high-ranking representatives from various interest groups, such as seniors, women, or underprivileged youth. In the district, anyway, it does not typically include the shady or nefarious lobbyists who are justifiably blamed for much of the rot and corruption that runs through contemporary American politics. Those folks ply their trade where real power resides; Washington, Sacramento, etc.

Nonetheless, covering many local events gave me a sense of the scope, range, reach, and necessity of government that I would not have had otherwise. I would gain much more insight into this phenomenon when I started working for politicians, beginning in the early 1990s.

On a Thursday morning in the spring of 1984, I was with a friend in my two-bedroom, $500 per month, rent-controlled North Hollywood apartment when the phone rang. It was my best friend on the *Tribune* reporting staff, Steve Tamaya (who we lost, sadly, in 1999 from a brain aneurysm at age 37). A week or so earlier, Steve and I had collaborated on an article detailing how the political cult led by Lyndon LaRouche had obtained the credit card information of various unsuspecting people and used it to make unauthorized contributions to the organization. We interviewed a LaRouche representative at the *Tribune* offices, who after an hour of amiable back and forth, refused to admit the transgression but also said he would talk to the organization about refunding the money to anyone who felt she had been duped; my word, not his. The story ran a couple days later, on the front page of the second section.

In my quest to finish the article, which was a minor scoop, I didn't think for a moment about any repercussions from its being published, other than a letter to the editor or two, even though LaRouche was running for president in 1984.

And then Steve called me.
"They're protesting," he whispered, in lieu of a greeting.
"Who's protesting?"
"The La Rouchies." For some reason, it's never LaRouchites, only LaRouchies.

"What do you mean, they're protesting?"

"A bunch of them are marching in front of the building carrying signs 'Waldman, KGB, Waldman, KGB."

I should mention that in the bizarre LaRouche hierarchy of evil, the KGB is right there with the Queen of England and the CIA. Part of me wanted to be in the newsroom, watching the demonstration against yours truly. After all, this was not an everyday occurrence in the life of a midlevel reporter at a midlevel publication.

But another part of me, the rational, sensible part, was glad to be 25 miles away. People who are willing to publicly accuse me of working for the KGB are capable of anything.

I thanked Steve for the information and hung up the phone, When I relayed the story to my companion, she got very excited, said it was just like *The Year of Living Dangerously*. I disagreed, though not with much conviction. For their part, the demonstrators never returned, apparently satisfied that they had made their point.

I spent nearly four years at the *Tribune*, leaving in December 1985 to take a position with the *Jewish Journal*, a new publication covering the huge Jewish community of Los Angeles, third-largest in the world. I was grateful for the *Tribune* job, not the least of which was because the reporters were required to produce several stories per week, which made me a better writer — focused and precise.

At the same time, I was also eager to start writing freelance articles about rock music. I was a regular and enthusiastic reader of *Rolling Stone, Creem, Circus,* and *Crawdaddy* and had a glamorous notion of what it meant to be a rock journalist: Free albums, free concert tickets, hanging out with musicians, foisting my strong opinions on Young America, all while achieving second-tier prestige, which might be sufficient to get a date or two with cute, smart, hip women from my generation. If I was not a viable candidate for full-time employment at one of these esteemed publications — lacking both the experience and connections — then I would find another place for my work. But first, I needed a subject.

The problem was twofold: dearth of ideas and lack of access. The major artists I preferred had been written about, many times over, and my obscure favorites might as well have been living in the outer reaches of the Solar System. It wasn't only that I didn't know anyone in rock and roll, I didn't know anyone who knew anyone. On top of that, I hadn't yet developed the guile and nerve to circumvent any real or imagined barriers. I wanted sources and subjects to drop into my lap, which was just another rock and roll fantasy.

Until the age of 23, my knowledge of rock and roll history was both extensive and conventional. I had read many relevant articles and books and listened to two lengthy AM radio specials devoted to the subject, one at the end of the 1960s and the other a decade later. These sources focused on the early interplay between the blues, country, and rhythm and blues; added a healthy dose of pop - *Bandstand* and the Brill building — and from 1964 forward, covered categories, primarily the British Invasion and Motown; monster acts, such as the Beatles, the Rolling Stones, and Elton John; and the stock 70s genres, singer/songwriter, funk, disco. I could and did absorb this stuff over and over, but after a while, it felt as if I wasn't learning anything new; a walking encyclopedia in need of a second edition.

This static situation was also complicating my effort to find something to write about. As a person who didn't even rise sufficiently to the level of "budding journalist," I had no choice but to propose a topic that had never—or rarely—been considered. Relying on my good name would get me nowhere.

The answer, when it came, was a direct result of my friendship with David Reyes. It turned out that rock and roll historians were no better than those in other fields at recognizing the contributions and achievements of Mexican Americans. With the exception of Ritchie Valens, who was just a footnote at the time, Mexican American and Chicano musicians (the term that achieved prominence at the end of the 1960s) had been ignored in the extensive library of rock and roll literature. I was selfishly grateful for the omission.

Through David, I learned about Ritchie Valens' astonishing productivity, and was introduced to Chan Romero, the Blendells, and the Romancers from the 1950s and the early 1960s; the Sisters, Mark and the Escorts, Cannibal and the Headhunters, Thee Midniters, and the Salas Brothers from the mid-1960s; and El Chicano, Tierra, Yaqui, and a then-rising band called Los Lobos from the end of the decade and into the early 1970s. Most of the Mexican-American rock groups hailed from Southern California, with the notable exceptions of Sam the Sham and the Pharaohs (Texas) and Question Mark and the Mysterians (Michigan). Even so, there were enough artists on my home turf to justify several articles, especially during a period when

American culture had finally taken note of Latinos. As I traveled in an aging Chevrolet Caprice and had no personal expense account, proximity was critical.

David would constantly play, for my benefit, selections from Mexican-American performers spanning the early 1950s to then-current times, the late 1970s. These groups and solo artists were heavily influenced by Black music of the day, Doo Wop and Motown, along with surf guitar, mid-1960s Rolling Stones, and later—various Latin styles and rhythms, which was both a political and musical decision. As evidenced by their choices, these artists were blissfully unencumbered by the categorizing and polarization that was beginning to take hold of the recording industry around 1967, the notorious distinction between white and Black music that was most apparent in radio playlists. Latino performers, their scrambling management, and the wider community adopted the sensible philosophy that in music the only distinction worth making was between good and bad. For this audience, especially the youth, ethnicity, gender, and race were irrelevant. It was the advantage of not having a personal stake in the Black/white divide.

No one was better at ranging across the pop music spectrum than Thee Midniters, a prolific and innovative seven-member group that cleverly adapted the fashions of the Beatles in *A Hard Day's Night*; charcoal suits, black ties, and black, Cuban-heel boots—the entire ensemble purchased at local shops in and around East Los Angeles. The local audience loved the look, bestowing upon the group the ultimate compliment: "Mexican Beatles."

Thee Midniters performed a range of styles, from "Strangers in the Night" to Doo Wop to blistering rock and roll to up-tempo soul, all on the same albums, displaying a level of skill and versatility that surpassed even the high expectations of their most dedicated fans. The group was also ahead of its time, incorporating a horn section years before Chicago and Blood Sweat & Tears thought of the idea. Because Thee Midniters—and all Mexican-American artists at that time—barely existed in the minds of middle (white) America, they were able to follow their own natural instincts without the interference of high-priced producers and major labels.

It also meant that few journalists had bothered to write about the group, which is where David and I stepped in. In early 1982, we pitched an article on Thee Midniters for *Goldmine,* a monthly publication then dedicated to rock and roll from the 1950s through the mid-1970s. The editor commissioned a piece, and David and I began a journalistic collaboration that would lead, 16 years later, to publication of our book, *Land of a Thousand Dances: Chicano Rock and Roll from Southern California.* Our various projects included, in 1997, the release of a three-CD series on the Rhino label entitled *Brown-Eyed Soul,* and serving as associate producers of the 60-minute documentary *Chicano Rock: The Sounds of East LA,* which aired nationally on PBS in December 2008. Both of us appear on camera in the film.

For the *Goldmine* piece, we interviewed three members of Thee Midniters in a brightly lit apartment located in Alhambra, a few miles east of downtown Los Angeles. David had called on one of his contacts, who provided us the number to a band member. When we got in touch with Roy Marquez, the lead guitar player, he not only agreed to do the interview, but promised to invite two of his colleagues. This pattern would be repeated through the years, as David and I interviewed — both together and separately — dozens of participants in the Chicano rock scene from Southern California. Musicians, producers, disc jockeys, and managers were not only eager to contribute, but generously offered to assist in any way possible. They were as grateful to have their stories told — finally — as we were grateful for their involvement.

At that time, spring of 1981, I toted around a black, hard plastic tape recorder the size of a block of wood, far too obtrusive and clunky to be ignored by interviewees. But the artists we recorded on that ridiculous, yet dependable, device were so eager to share their stories that its presence proved to be no obstacle.

After the *Goldmine* article appeared, David and I continued our personal research into the subject of Chicano rock and roll while also trying to come up with other writing possibilities. Because of the article, we were occasionally called upon to speak to college and high school classes with mostly Latino students. These presentations, which included photos and music, also encouraged us to seek other possibilities.

Toward the end of the 1980s, we came up with the idea of devoting an entire book to the subject. Though the decision seems obvious now, at that time neither of us had any sense how to do a book. I would serve as the principal writer — David was co-researcher and archivist, the possessor of extraordinary photo and record collections — yet the only thing I had ever written over 15 pages was my journalism school master's thesis on how major newspapers covered the U.S. economic crisis of 1974–1975. I had spent an entire year agonizing over that assignment, even though it was heavily reliant on footnotes.

In the early 1990s, I finally got around to writing a proposal and three chapters, which I had been told was the publishing industry standard. We assembled a package that included text and a collection of David's photos. Fortunately, a longtime friend of my parents, Julie Popkin, had recently started her own literary agency. Julie generously agreed to shop the product, which spared two untested authors the disappointment and frustration of having to find their own agent.

In 1995, Julie succeeded in placing the book with the University of New Mexico Press, an obvious choice for the subject matter, but one that would never have occurred to me. I was understandably elated on the day that I received the news. I was going to be an author, which was something that I had never considered, even though I was a steady, at times, voracious reader, not to mention proud possessor of a master's in journalism. On the following day, my mood changed completely. I panicked, asking myself a series of debilitating questions that fell under the general heading: "Who the hell do you think you are writing a book?" Around midnight, after my wife and child had fallen asleep, I got into my car in Sherman Oaks and drove the entire length of Ventura Boulevard, nearly 12 miles, which at that hour on a Sunday was a mix of bright lights, few vehicles, and blocks of closed businesses, except for a smattering of 24-hour coffee shops and bars. I appreciated the urban solitude, which helped calm me for what was to come.

Over the next few years, I developed a regimen of writing an hour or 90 minutes in the evening, after arriving home from my day job — press secretary and district director for Congressman Howard Berman. David and I were simultaneously continuing to conduct interviews across Southern California, experiencing the double pleasure of locating hard-to-find performers and actually sitting down with them. Some of these efforts yielded unexpected success. We gave up trying to connect with one singer known by the street nickname of Scar, former member of Cannibal and the Headhunters, after learning that he had died. "I heard that rumor, too," he told David and me, upon showing up unannounced at a group interview.

Our subjects willingly shared their stories and provided a wealth of material; snapshots, news articles, flyers, and posters. A member of the Headhunters even showed us crinkly Polaroid photos of him and his colleagues on the plane with members of a certain popular group from Liverpool when they toured together in the late summer of 1965. Some of the people we interviewed produced for our enjoyment items that were literally stored in shoe boxes and tucked away on the top shelf of crowded closets. They never expected that anyone would want to see the stuff, let alone interview them for a book.

Land of a Thousand Dances: Chicano Rock and Roll from Southern California (University of New Mexico Press) was published in the spring of 1998. Although not an oral history, the text is guided by the stories of the many and varied artists who fashioned a bona fide Chicano rock and roll scene, which was mostly (but not exclusively) centered in East Los Angeles and neighboring Boyle Heights. In addition to the music, the book discusses culture and politics, especially after 1967, when the burgeoning Chicano movement merged with growing community opposition to the war in Vietnam.

Though Mexican-American/Chicano rock and roll produced no stars — other than Ritchie Valens — and a few hit singles, it served as a vivid, four-decade example of the extent to which rock and roll permeated youth culture. From 1962 to 1968, dozens of teenaged groups gathered in garages to spend their afternoons learning singles — many of them obscure — that they heard on soul and rhythm and blues radio stations in Southern California. On occasion, these covers achieved their own national success, most notably Cannibal and the Headhunters' version of "Land of a Thousand Dances," which kicks off with the famous chant of "Na, na, na, na, na...." and the Premiers' interpretation of "Farmer John" (1964), heavily influenced by "Louie, Louie."

In the three years following publication of the book, David and I held dozens of readings and signings at bookstores, high schools, libraries, and colleges across Southern California. We often invited musicians featured in the book to share their stories and, in some cases, perform. We treated these appearances as an opportunity to expose audiences — which were primarily but not exclusively Latino — to performers that they more than likely had never seen.

A month after the book was published, an editor/friend suggested that I contact a documentarian named Jon Wilkman, who specialized in LA-based subjects. It took me only a few minutes to convince Jon that the history of Chicano rock and roll deserved to be told on film. At the end of our first conversation, he said that I shouldn't expect the documentary to air for 10 years, which was apparently typical for the medium. I murmured my assent, but silently thought that timeframe sounded ridiculous. After all, the book had taken only three years to write, including the proposal. As it happened, Jon was short by six months: The documentary aired in December 2008.

A few months before the broadcast, I had contacted UNM Press to let it know that a film based on our book was scheduled to air. The editor I spoke with said that sounded like a very good reason to publish a second edition. Not surprisingly, I agreed with him. The new cover featured a famous painting by the Chicano artist George Yepes, entitled "La Serenata," which depicts a mournful skeleton playing a guitar, and an updated introduction that discussed performers from the early 2000s, including Quetzal and Lysa Flores. The book is still in print to this day, 2022.

In 2016, we found another medium for telling a story grounded in Chicano rock and roll, when the musical *Eastside Heartbeats* debuted at Casa 0101 Theatre in Boyle Heights. I wrote the script for *Heartbeats*, which was based on the true story of Cannibal and the Headhunters' opening for the Beatles at the Hollywood Bowl in 1965. I will discuss the musical at greater length in Chapter 23. Not a bad body of work for two guys from much different circumstances who happened to meet at Tower Records in West Covina, California, in 1978.

CHAPTER 19

"Try To Remember"

The Fantasticks, 1960

Before I was hired as a reporter at the *San Gabriel Valley Tribune*, I wrote theater reviews for the paper, $25 per submission. On a whim, I had simply called the arts editor one day and asked if he needed someone to perform that service. I told him that I was a student at the USC School of Journalism and had written a couple of freelance concert reviews for a free paper called *BAM*, which stood for Bay Area Music. The arts editor said my credentials sounded fine, he needed a reviewer to cover local theater, and asked whether I could start the following week. "Yes indeed," I responded. Sometimes, it's that easy.

The stint began in June 1980 and lasted nearly two years. I was usually assigned to review community theater productions of popular musicals from the 1940s, 1950s, and 1960s, which I hadn't anticipated. Yet, the experience cured me of an arrogant yet juvenile bias toward that genre.

Prior to becoming a reviewer, I had scrupulously avoided musicals, without any empirical evidence believing them to be phony, overwrought, simple-minded, and trite. Who but unenlightened audiences could take seriously characters singing their thoughts, while gazing skyward, fists clenched, wearing on their faces that ridiculous "I'll never quit" look of determination?

I was also ticked off at musical theater for making a mockery of an art form that included Beckett, Chekov, and Shakespeare. It was like throwing the Carpenters in with Jimi Hendrix and calling all of it pop music. Out of respect to Real Theater, and in maintaining faith with my literary aspirations, I was condescending, and elitist towards musicals, the whole lot of them. I refused to even argue the point.

Still, I couldn't very well condemn musicals for the simple reason that they were musicals. I had to give each production a chance. Anything else would have been blatantly unfair, if not immoral.

My first assignment was a performance of *The Fantasticks*, which was being staged in the basement of a church in the city of Pomona. A few years earlier, I had ridiculed an actor friend for attending a production of that same show, merely because the title sounded cloying and pretentious, an encapsulation of everything I despised about musical theater. Now here I was in the audience for, wouldn't you know it, *The Fantasticks*. Even worse, I had to write about the performance, while keeping an open mind.

I took a seat near the front of the stage, which lacked a curtain, placed on an accompanying chair the notebook I had remembered to bring and my first-ever press packet. I wore a blazer, which seemed to me appropriate attire for The Critic. I refused to take off the coat even though the space provided little relief from a late June heat wave. I was willing to endure personal discomfort to preserve my Broadway fantasy, although the audience numbered maybe 35 in a room that could hold twice that many.

The lights dimmed, the music began, and a man in his 40s walked on to the stage wearing a black hat with a black chinstrap, a royal blue shirt with puffed sleeves, and black pants. He looked like the quintessential Spanish matador. I had read nothing about the show, an unforgivable omission that I would correct with experience. As a result, I didn't expect to be sitting 20 feet from a figure that reminded me of Zorro.

But when the actor started to sing, all my misgivings about his character, his costume, and the musical form itself disappeared. In a stirring baritone — the kind of voice that even gives goose bumps to cynical rookie critics — he performed a number called "Try to Remember." I was absolutely stunned. I had heard a version of this song, many years earlier, on an AM radio station in the Bay Area. I was haunted then by the melody and the words, even though I was too young to understand the bittersweet attractions of youthful love and romance. I didn't catch the song's title, however, and had been attempting without success to find it for years.

Now I was hearing it again, live and on stage, a gorgeous interpretation. The sheer surprise of encountering this beautiful melody from my distant past ended in an instant my harsh and illogical resistance to musicals. As soon as the number finished, I wanted to hear it all over again; for the rest of the evening, if possible. (The character, who is actually the narrator El Gallo, does perform a shortened version at the end.)

I am probably not the only person among the millions who have seen *The Fantasticks* since 1960 who have felt that way. Still, the show is more than a one-hit wonder. I enjoyed many of the songs, which blended the sounds of late 1950s pop, jazz, and folk, and got caught up in the story of Matt and Louisa. Leaving the church that night, I even contemplated the once unthinkable; buying the soundtrack of the Off-Broadway production. I eventually decided against it, but only because there were so many rock and soul albums I needed to add to my burgeoning collection.

It would be inaccurate to say I became a genuine fan of musicals after seeing this production, but you could certainly put me in the category of the newly curious. As a weekly reviewer of Community Theater, I was in an ideal position to have my curiosity satisfied. That summer I attended performances of *Dames at Sea*, *Finian's Rainbow*, and *South Pacific*, among others. Over the next two years, as I continued reviewing for the *San Gabriel Valley Tribune* and also became a freelancer for an LA-based zine called *Drama-Logue*, I reviewed numerous musicals, including *I Do! I Do!*, another product from the creators of *The Fantasticks*, and an original work written and composed by a local university drama professor about strange doings in late 1930s Latvia.

By this point, I was a true devotee of musicals, not only dancing, singing, and plot, but the form as well. Increasing exposure had worn down my elitist resistance to the idea that a convincing, powerful message can emerge from the proper blend of story and song, or that a genre reliant on spectacle is incapable of producing something moving and real. I often experienced chills watching a high-spirited number, and occasionally got teary during scenes of sadness or resilience, a daring admission for a seemingly unflappable critic. I was like the young Tom Waldman who cried at the end of *The Wizard of Oz*.

If only I had discovered musicals earlier! As the reviewer was always allotted two tickets to a performance, I held in my hands a valuable calling card. I invited other female Tower employees to accompany me to musicals, plus women I met in school and other places. On the rare occasions I was turned down, it was with deep regrets, the person otherwise engaged making me promise that I would give her another chance. Perhaps Henry Kissinger is right, and "Power is the ultimate aphrodisiac." Still, being a theater critic with a pair of tickets ranks in the Top 10.

Thirty-five years later, I wrote my own musical, *Eastside Heartbeats*, which had two sold-out runs at a theater in the Boyle Heights section of Los Angeles and was profiled in the Sunday entertainment section of the *Los Angeles Times*. Writing the musical would likely have never happened but for my stint as a weekend theater reviewer with the *San Gabriel Valley Tribune*.

CHAPTER 20

"Everything I Own"

Bread, 1972

I stood in the middle of a packed library square at the Claremont Colleges, surrounded by people with personal memories of the New Deal and World War II. Although it was a Monday morning, I knew that the crowd would be arriving early. Ronald Reagan, the 1980 Republican presidential nominee, was hugely popular in most of the white majority communities across California. Fourteen years earlier, he had been elected governor of the state in a stunning landslide, and if anything, his appeal had only increased ever since. Today, he was making a campaign appearance in Claremont, and I was there, the first time I had ever attended a speech by a presidential candidate of any party.

I wanted to see Reagan in person for the same reason I had tickets to see Bruce Springsteen at the Los Angeles Sports Arena in a few weeks: I heard he put on a great show. Although I liked the Boss far more than the Gipper, I was not among the multitudes who made up his adoring base. I thought he was a bit too earnest in his embrace of the healing power of rock and roll. I preferred my performers to be slightly cynical and remote; the English, for example. I didn't have to see Springsteen in concert the way I had to see Led Zeppelin in March 1975 and the Rolling Stones three months later. But I also knew that attending a Springsteen show would add luster to my rock and roll resume, not to mention provide great entertainment.

As we waited for the candidate to appear, I became aware that numerous students had arrived, a few hundred yards behind me. It was unclear whether they had deliberately chosen that distant spot, with its obstructed view of the stage, or had been steered there by event organizers and security. Many of the students were dressed in blue jeans and t-shirts and they carried signs, which for the moment remained at their sides. You didn't have to be a political junkie to draw the conclusion that this group was probably not going to vote for Reagan in November.

There was still no sign of the featured guest when a man in his early 30s, well-groomed and wearing a suit the shade of patriotic blue approached the microphone to make an announcement: "Ladies and Gentlemen, please give a warm welcome to David Gates." Had I heard him correctly? David Gates, leader of the soft-rock group Bread, which had several major hits between 1970 and 1974? I never expected this opening act from the Reagan campaign, even in a college town. Although Bread wasn't exactly Alice Cooper, the group certainly had more pop culture cachet than the artists you'd hear on the Adult Contemporary stations. I naturally assumed that the Reagan campaign would avoid even a marginal association with contemporary American pop. Why mess with a winning formula? Hadn't Reagan achieved great success campaigning against hippies, drugs, and student protestors?

I presumed that by agreeing to appear, Gates was publicly declaring his support for the Republican candidate. I found that a bit odd, but only because Reagan's showbiz backers that I knew of were Hollywood veterans such as Buddy Ebsen, Hugh O'Brian, Robert Stack, and Jimmy Stewart. Still, I had never subscribed to the idea — promoted by the left and right for their own purposes — that all rock or soft rock performers were by definition left-wing radicals, liberals, or even Democrats. Rock was invented in America, and by the end of the 1970s had become a multibillion dollar industry. What could be more red, white, and blue than that?

The singer/songwriter walked to the front of the podium, carrying his acoustic guitar, and waved to the crowd, as if this were just another gig. I temporarily forgot the main reason I had come to the rally and shifted my position to get a better view of the stage. I had not purchased any Bread singles or albums, but I liked a few of the group's songs, and I hoped that Gates would include them in his set, even under such unlikely conditions. If he were playing a free concert in Claremont for any reason, I would have attended.

The guy didn't disappoint, performing excellent solo versions of "Everything I Own," and "Guitar Man," my two favorites. The entire show lasted maybe 20 minutes. At the end, I applauded, putting aside partisanship for the moment and proving yet again the trite observation that music brings people together. Even members of the Glenn Miller Generation seemed satisfied with the set.

Reagan took the stage about half an hour later, to great applause. Although he was 69 years old, which seemed ancient in an era still defined by Kennedy vigor, he came across as energetic and engaged, squelching the "age issue" before our very eyes. If it was all an act, then no wonder Hollywood took a chance on him. In his remarks, Reagan stressed familiar themes: The perils of Big Government, and the humiliation inflicted on America by the ongoing Iranian hostage situation, which precipitated a second energy crisis, including long lines at the gas pump. He had tried these ideas out across the country, to great success. Why should Claremont be any different?

When Reagan arrived at the end of his speech, or what seemed to be the end, he suddenly adopted a more conversational tone, as if he was veering from the main presentation. "I heard those demonstrators yelling 'Heil, Reagan," said the candidate, gesturing with his head toward the back of the expansive square, where the student protestors were situated. He paused for a moment before delivering the big payoff. "If it hadn't been for my generation, they would be yelling Heil, somebody else."

The roar from the nonstudent section far exceeded the decibel level generated by the anti-Carter, pro-USA applause lines littered throughout the speech. It was the sound of thousands of older conservatives, ecstatic to hear disrespectful and slovenly youths dismissed with cheery contempt. They had been waiting for this moment since 1965.

I barely heard the students at all, let alone chanting "Heil, Reagan," although I was situated only a few hundred years in front of them. Perhaps my hearing was inferior to Reagan's, who was born in 1911. Or perhaps the campaign wrote its own ending, the perfect signoff to an appearance in a college town filled with members of the academic elite. It could have been the case that belligerent undergraduates at a different campus yelled "Heil, Reagan" and the team decided to keep that in the script whenever the candidate encountered any organized opposition at a progressive institution of higher learning.

Despite the evident charm, a toned-down version of Barry Goldwater, Reagan's persona and success unleashed a new wave of obnoxious, pugnacious conservatism, *The Charge of The White Brigade*.

I witnessed it firsthand at USC in September 1984. I was, by then, working as a reporter for *The San Gabriel Valley Tribune* assigned to cover a campaign speech by the Democratic nominee for president, Walter Mondale. The event was set for the center of campus, next to the statue of Tommy Trojan, the famous symbol of USC virility. Before Mondale appeared, dozens of red-faced, muscular white guys assembled around the edge of the designated area, eyeing the gathering crowd with scary looks of contempt and hatred. They seemed to resent the fact that the vice president under the disgraced Jimmy Carter would deign to run against their hero, President Ronald Reagan.

These knuckleheads saw it as their sacred duty to disrupt the appearance, and in vile fashion. Mondale had barely begun his remarks when they started yelling "USA,

USA" in rapid cadence, as if the Democratic candidate was an Olympic team representing some despised third-world country. The speaker was forced to continuously raise his voice, and eventually to take note of the obstructionists, though you could tell he hated having to do so. They ignored his pointed remarks and continued their thuggish behavior.

Although I didn't know it at the time, I was witnessing the ugly future of American conservatism. Reagan's political progeny did not do justice to either his name or reputation. Within little more than a decade, Rush Limbaugh had become the most popular radio talk show host in America, Newt Gingrich and his group would take control of the House of Representatives, and Fox News came on the air. In 2016, the GOP openly courted white supremacists. The lunatics no longer represented the fringe.

I accept the premise that there is a connection between the dominance of Reagan in the 1980s and the revival of the bullying, terrifying, deeply cynical right wing that has been a critical part of American political life for three decades. I have seen on television the same crazed look and overly aggressive manner displayed by people attending Trump rallies that I saw on the faces of those goons at USC. Still, it wasn't always this way. On a cool October morning in 1980, David Gates played a string of his serene, melodic pop hits on acoustic guitar while the crowd waited for Reagan. It's absolutely impossible to imagine the equivalent at a Trump rally.

CHAPTER 21

"Starting Over"

John Lennon, 1980

I decided John Lennon was my favorite Beatle well after the group broke up. I arose one day in the mid-1970s and realized I liked more of his songs than I did the songs written by Paul or George. I had never paid attention to compositional differences between the Beatles before. But in my late teens I realized that John had a way of invoking a range of moods and a particular milieu that I found especially appealing. "I'm Only Sleeping" was a tribute to an acutely male form of indifferent resignation; "She Said She Said" was a funky satire of cosmic gibberish; "Doctor Robert" allowed sheltered youths like me the chance to gaze into the abyss of New York decadence; "Strawberry Fields Forever" was *about* me ("Living is easy with eyes closed, misunderstanding all you see"); "Good Night" was a beautiful melody, wholly unexpected after the biting wit and introspection that characterized Lennon's songs on the *White Album*. It seemed back then that he could do anything.

I was far less enthusiastic about his solo work, even the much-beloved "Imagine," which struck me as trite, a word I would never have used to describe even his lesser Beatle efforts. I took the same attitude toward most of the records released by the individual members, with the exception of George's *All Things Must Pass*, my choice for the best post-Beatles, solo Beatle LP; a triple album, with a memorable, gnomelike cover. Without speculating as to the reasons, let's just politely say that in each case the second career did not measure up to the first.

Still, I felt cheated when John all but disappeared from the music scene between 1976 and the first part of 1980. In the mid-1970s, I had started to think about rock music and culture in general differently from before, adding the questions "What is it that this person is trying to say and why?" to the more fundamental "Is this song, or play, or film good or bad?" Since I knew the lyrics to nearly all Beatle songs, it was a good place to begin my own cultural awakening. John tended to be the more poetic lyricist in the group and therefore the most fun for a college-educated kid who wanted to write criticism. I studied his songs from *Rubber Soul* forward, for the first time focusing on words rather than instrumentation. Most of his images I understood, or thought I understood, on my first reading. When he was at his most obscure, I applied my own idiosyncratic interpretation, and didn't worry about whether it was "accurate," whatever that might mean.

My foray into "Lennonology" had the unintended effect of wishing that he was recording again, and in the news. As I mentioned, I was indifferent toward his individual work, but I was now curious about what he might come up with next. Part of this was pure selfishness on my part; rock was entering its late-70s slump, with even punk on the wane. I didn't expect Lennon to save the music by any means (as the Beatles had done 15 years earlier) but a new JL release would at least stave off the boredom and give us something to talk about.

And then, in the fall of 1980, Lennon did put out an album, called *Double Fantasy*, which featured a jacket photo that made him look 25. I liked the title song, which achieved its intent of mixing a 1950s vibrato vocal and strong rhythm guitar — think of Gene Vincent or Eddie Cochran — with a clean, insistent, contemporary production. Lennon did a number of interviews, including with the *Los Angeles Times* and *Playboy*, mainly to promote the album, though he also spoke at great length about the legacy of the Beatles, including the songs, exactly what I had hoped would happen if and when he re-emerged.

Around 10 p.m. PST on Monday, December 8, 1980, my sports-writing class at USC had just ended, and I headed toward my car for the 25-mile drive to Duarte, where my girlfriend Diane lived. The campus seemed subdued, more than usual, but I didn't attribute it to anything other than Monday evening repose. I got into my car, the same '67 Chevy Caprice on loan from my parents, fastened the seat belt, and turned on an oldies rock and roll station, the usual routine. The DJ, a kindly middle-aged man named Brother John, was reporting that John Lennon had been shot and killed by a gunman in New York who wore a smirk when being led away by police.

It's a strange thing to receiving shocking news in the middle of a freeway commute. For one, there is the responsibility you have to the other drivers. I suddenly felt deflated and devastated, bereft of spirit, soul, and sustenance; all liquid, no mass. I wanted to fall into bed, face down, and try to absorb that which could not be absorbed. This was not a realistic option while traveling 60 MPH on a Southern California freeway. I had to keep my eyes on the road, hands on the wheel, the rules that I learned in driver training back in '72. I turned the dial to another station, not for additional confirmation — I believed Brother John — but for further details and reflection. The DJ, a dude with one of those mellow and self-assured on-air voices that defined FM rock in the 60s and 70s, said that the murder of John Lennon was "not a very cosmic thing to have happened." I wasn't entirely sure what that meant, but it sounded right, or at least it sounded right for this audience.

I wondered what people were thinking in the cars around me on the eastbound San Bernardino Freeway. There were no obvious signs of grief or despair. Drivers were not honking their horns, perhaps because of the safety implications, and I didn't see any people visibly upset, as I quickly glanced through their windows. I presumed that, like me, they were keeping their emotions in check for now to avoid accidents.

I turned the radio dial to the "all news, all the time" station on AM. The announcer said that the shooting occurred around 11 p.m. New York time, and that the victim died almost immediately. Hearing these details, I felt cheated and stupid, as if the world had been deliberately withholding a secret from me. For an hour, I sat in sports-writing class unaware that my favorite Beatle had been murdered. Nobody bothered to tell us. I deplore how technology dominates our lives in the 21st century, but had the crime happened 30 years in the future, I would have received several texts as soon as the news was reported, made equal to my in-the-know peers.

When I arrived at my girlfriend's place she was distraught, yet dry-eyed. We turned on the television. Crowds of people had gathered in Central Park, near the scene of the murder. Some were crying, some were singing Lennon songs, all of them appeared to be in various stages of emotional disarray. As a nation, we were certainly not unaccustomed to the killing by gunfire of famous people, but who thought that such a fate would befall a member of the Beatles?

A theme soon took hold, which smacked of 60s self-importance, less about the victim and his widow and son, than the fans. You heard and read that the killer "Blew away my youth" or "Killed the dream." Lacking any sense of irony, the people who peddled this nonsense didn't realize that in a perverse way they had found something good in the murder, because it forced them to finally grow up. They wouldn't agree, of course, but instead continue to bemoan the horrible twist of fate that intruded on their sacred memories. Facing adulthood with courage and honesty was not an option, because getting old or older was not part of the plan.

The morning after the ex-Beatles were reduced to three I worked the midday shift at Tower Records. I knew even before arriving to work that we would be playing nothing but Lennon's solo music and Beatle records all day. Radio stations had set the programming agenda the night before.

To do anything different would be interpreted as disrespect, callousness, or monumental stupidity.

It was a tribute, but not a celebration of life. We played the music at a lower volume than usual, even for a Tuesday afternoon. I heard the songs differently that day, and for weeks afterward, ambivalence and uncertainty replaced enthusiasm and familiarity. I wondered if I could ever listen to the Beatles and Lennon again under any conditions. The music made me think of the murder, of course, and I didn't need any more reminders of the horrible crime. But it went deeper than that, a sense of loss that somehow tainted the entire catalogue. I had no hesitation listening to the Doors, Jimi Hendrix, Janis Joplin, or Elvis, but I quickly realized it would not be the same with the Beatles, who even in "death," especially in death, were larger than life. I would need to work my way through the grief and pain before I could contemplate getting back to where I once belonged.

A record store is about the best place to mourn a fallen rock star, and it's also among the worst. I was grateful to be in the company of my somber, hurting colleagues, sharing memories and providing a public service. This was far preferable to mourning Lennon on my own, or as part of some whipped-up classroom discussion of his art and legacy.

A Tower salesclerk was also required to help on the floor. I had always tried to show customers a modicum of respect, even if their manners were brusque and their tastes appalling. I maintained a veneer of cordiality, resisted the urge to pass harsh judgment, including the most difficult cases, surly and uninformed. As I reminded myself, it was not my job to improve the listening habits of the American public.

On December 9, 1980, and throughout the following week, everyone was a fan of John Lennon's. I saw this firsthand at Tower, and at times it disgusted me. Some of the people asking for the former Beatle's records acted like they had never heard of him before. I recall in particular a woman approaching the counter with her boyfriend and inquiring in an uncertain voice if we had any records by "Lennon," as if she was unsure of his first name. I silently pointed her in the direction of two massive stacks of *Double Fantasy*.

I probably should not have taken personally the sudden interest in Lennon by this woman and other men and women like her whom I encountered at Tower during the next week. I didn't need to add their rude ignorance—as I saw it—to my emotional anguish. In that stripped-down, American way, they had a "right" to remember Lennon in any manner they chose. After all, the sensational death of a famous person elicits a range of responses that are played out in public. In August 1977, the world witnessed garish scenes in front of Graceland as thousands mourned the death of Elvis Presley. Nothing close followed the murder of Lennon, which was a relief.

It was also selfish of me to hope that everyone would regard the life and death of John Lennon in a way that I deemed acceptable. Of course, my proprietary interest was driven by an intimate connection to his music. I took it personally when certain people did not pay proper homage to the guy who wrote "Baby, You're a Rich Man" and "I Am the Walrus." In my opinion, it would have been better if they simply didn't acknowledge his monumental contributions and shocking death. But nobody appointed me to oversee the grieving process.

After a few months, I was able to listen to the Beatles and Lennon solo unencumbered by an immediate association with the murder. In that sense, normalcy returned, although I would never stop wishing the madman's gun had misfired.

CHAPTER 22

Bach, Beethoven, and Mozart

17th–19th Centuries

On September 10, 2001, I flew from Los Angeles to Washington, DC, on business. At the time I served as the communications manager for the Los Angeles branch of the Federal Reserve Bank of San Francisco. I had been looking forward for weeks to working with my colleagues at the Fed's Board of Governors, and maybe meeting Alan Greenspan, then revered as the genius behind America's economic boom.

During the ultra-smooth flight, I read an entire issue of *Vanity Fair*, even the perfumed ads, and watched *Bridget Jones' Diary*, which I enjoyed more than I had expected. A few hours after landing, I accompanied a friend to dinner at a boisterous steak and beer place filled with cocky young conservatives, male and female, still ecstatic over the U.S. Supreme Court's decision in Bush v. Gore. I despised our blueblood president and his affected Texas twang, turned away from the TV whenever he appeared on the screen. Back in Southern California, everyone I knew felt the same way. But that night I entered a different country, surrounded by people who adored "GW" and were ecstatic to be done with the Clintons.

I awoke the next morning at 6:30 a.m., which was really 3:30 a.m., determined to get in a 45-minute workout before my first meeting. I was staying at the Capitol Hill Hyatt, closest to Congressional office buildings, and a gym with the latest equipment. I found a digitized lifecycle, chose 30 minutes, and pushed "manual" for my workout. To my right and left, middle-aged men wearing sports glasses were peddling furiously while reading the *New York Times* or *The Washington Post.*

I returned to my room, showered, dressed, and headed downstairs to the hotel restaurant. I promptly ordered a fancy omelet, one of my few indulgences on business travel. The three television sets in the lobby, volume at high levels, were all tuned to ABC's *Good Morning America.* The single channel made me suspicious; were the company's executives or lobbyists staying at the hotel? Coming from well outside the beltway, I believed that everything in Washington happened for a reason.

I first learned from Peter Jennings that something was wrong. In his calm, Canadian-tinged accent, the anchor person interrupted some breezy segment to announce that it appeared an airplane had collided with the World Trade Center in New York. A live camera shot showed thick, black smoke coming from the midsection of a massive structure. All around me, male diners pulled cell phones from their suit coat pockets, like Secret Service agents immediately brandishing weapons at the sound of gunfire. I hadn't yet processed the news, and these guys were already in contact with their families or the home office.

Then, the second plane hit, and even I realized that the nation was under attack. My first thought was the same one I have when I awake with a scratchy throat; should I go to work? Did a monstrous act of domestic terrorism constitute a legitimate excuse for staying away? If it had happened while I was in California, I would have been seriously conflicted. But traveling at taxpayers' expense I felt that I must honor my professional responsibilities, especially given the circumstances.

Outside the entrance to the hotel, dozens of people were nervously pacing, trying to plan their next move. At the curb, cab drivers eagerly beckoned potential riders; under capitalism, one person's fear is another person's opportunity. Although the weather was gorgeous, perfect for walking, I hailed a taxi, seeking the security of an enclosed space. During the drive, the all-news station playing on the cab's radio reported that a third plane had crashed into the Pentagon. Not more than a minute later, I saw a solid line of black smoke drift across the cloudless blue sky, which I still believe originated with the downed airliner.

When I arrived at the Federal Reserve, groups of people, confused and upset, were being kept from the facility by agitated security personnel, who had no more knowledge of the developing situation than the rest of us. Whatever else the terrorists hoped to accomplish, they had managed to foment chaos outside the world's most important financial institution, supposedly the model of order and stability. Yet, at that moment the DC Fed resembled a big box department store during the holiday season, security busily shooing customers out at closing.

My intentions were good, but going to work was out of the question, at least on 9/11. Rather than take another cab, I decided to walk the two miles back to my hotel, in part to gauge responses on the ground. I watched bureaucrats exiting federal buildings en masse, nervous and scared, professional planners without a plan, administrators of regulations and rules in the unfamiliar position of waiting for directives, although none were forthcoming. The immense power of the federal government had been reduced to confused men in white shirts and ties and women in business suits departing in chaos for their suburban homes.

As I walked along clogged sidewalks, people passing each other in desperate retreat, the thought occurred to me that I was witnessing an American version of Dunkirk. Of course, we were not being bombed or strafed while toting machine guns and heavy backpacks. Running from hidden terrorists is not comparable to running from the Luftwaffe. But part of the joy of being an amateur historian is finding tentative connections between remote events.

One immediate narrative, in place by 9/12, was that due to the attacks, "Everything had changed." Maybe for some, but not those who were poor, powerless, and neglected. Throughout the week, outside my hotel window, I saw homeless people lying under tattered sleeping bags or soiled boxes and heard them yelling at each other and at the world. In Washington, DC, the homeless live within sight of a multi-trillion dollar government that somehow can't find the means or will to help them. These men and women were exhausted, exposed, and hungry before the events of 9/11, and they would remain so during the patriotic aftermath and beyond.

I did spend parts of three days working at the Federal Reserve alongside accommodating staff, on makeshift projects, not being able to get back to Los Angeles until Sunday, September 16th. On Thursday, I heard Greenspan's unmistakable voice in an adjoining hallway, but I didn't actually see him, let alone shake his hand. He had other things on his mind, like reassuring millions of exceedingly nervous investors.

Throughout that week at the Capitol Hill Hyatt departing guests outnumbered new arrivals by at least 20 to 1. By Friday, September 14, I had the gym to myself. I spent an inordinate amount of time talking to hotel staff, many of whom came from foreign countries with histories of internal violence, war without end. I noticed that in the midst of this national crisis they smiled more than the native-born Americans and were friendlier, too. Unburdened by the idea of the American Exception, they had long ago adopted a clear-eyed strategy for coping with man-made disasters. I watched and learned, grateful for their examples.

On the afternoon before I flew home, I was listening to the local classical music station and trying to nap. I had been introduced to Bach, Beethoven, Brahms, Chopin, Handel, Haydn, Mozart, and more (including opera) by my father and mother. It seemed as if there was always classical music on in the house, although neither of my parents played an instrument. My proud father often shared with me the story that at the age of 3 or 4, I correctly identified Beethoven, or "Toven," in my toddler pronunciation, as the composer of a symphony I heard over the speakers in our living room.

Starting in high school, two of my closest friends were classical musicians. One played the piano and became a professor of music; the other, a violinist, became a lawyer. They reconnected me to classical music, and I even purchased the occasional album. But between the time of "Toven" and my late teens my listening skills had narrowed.

I had become so enamored of the qualities of rock, pop, and soul—beat, melody, guitar licks, and lyrics—that I had great difficulty adjusting to contemplative mode. I was a distinctly impatient listener, even to a seven-minute song in the art rock vernacular. I still don't know how I made it through the Yes concert in 1974 that I attended with my brother and his friend, except I was the guy with the driver's license. Except for a couple of obligatory hits performed at the end, the entire three-hour performance was devoted to the four songs, one per side, off of the recently released double album, *Tales from Topographic Oceans*. I spent a lot of the time with my head in my hands, which could be interpreted many ways, including intense concentration, I suppose.

I usually read when I listened to classical music, which was not exactly fair to the composers who had worked so hard on my behalf. But I was too impatient and immature to give symphonies, piano concertos, or string quartets the attention that they so obviously deserved. During my 40s and 50s, I refined my habits, and listened with active interest, even separating in my mind the various components of a particular piece. In 2012, I attended a four-hour, no intermission performance of the Philip Glass opera *Einstein on the Beach*. As with "She Loves You," a hundred other pop songs, or "Try to Remember," I was seduced from the opening notes, and didn't leave my seat once during the entire production.

On the warm afternoon of September 15, 2001, I sprawled on my hotel bed and opted for classical music. Apparently the public radio station sensed my mood. After one piece finished, the announcer spoke in calm, clear, and intimate tones and asked "Don't we all need to relax right now?" Although I appreciated his concern, I wondered: "Has this guy never heard Wagner?"

CHAPTER 23 (BONUS TRACK I)

"Hey Baby, They're Playing Our Song"

The Buckinghams, 1967

In July 2011, I started a job as communications director of the Los Angeles Unified School District, second largest in the nation to New York. A week or so after I took the position, the superintendent's top aide told me that my responsibilities included overseeing the district's television station, KLCS. This was not some storefront operation, as might be the case with smaller school districts, but the only PBS outlet in Los Angeles, which was housed in an expansive, dusty studio within walking distance of LAUSD headquarters.

At that point, I had appeared on television 10 to 15 times, usually to talk about my books, either *Land of a Thousand Dances* or *We All Want to Change the World: Rock and Politics from Elvis to Eminem.*

I loved the drama that accompanied TV appearances; nervous green room chit chat in the dwindling minutes before broadcast, and the actual taping, reminding myself to speak slowly and stay close to the topic. Although I didn't initially reveal my hidden agenda, my executive role with the station created the perfect opportunity to host a program that I had fantasized about for years. It even had a working title: *Rock and Roll Stories*.

The concept was simple; musicians selected five songs that mattered most to them, in advance of the taping. Over the course of an hour, the guest and I would engage in a wide-ranging discussion about his or her career and music in general, the exchanges interspersed with comments about the specific selections. These songs would be played at intervals throughout the program, for the musical benefit of host, guest, and viewers. I have always loved hearing or reading musicians discuss the artists and sounds that heavily influenced them and prompted their decision to drop everything in pursuit of a high risk career. My substantial library of rock books included several volumes of interviews that I would reread just for that moment when a budding performer came into contact with the song or artist that changed everything.

I pitched the idea to the station's general manager, who was actually my employee. She gave her approval. I then informed the Superintendent, who was actually my employer. He assented as well, mainly because he recognized the educational value, although it also didn't hurt that he was a huge rock and roll fan, who loved to tell us, his team, about historic concerts he'd attended.

Having secured the needed approvals, I set about booking guests. The first, Wayne Kramer, I approached after an event in his honor at the Grammy Museum in downtown Los Angeles. I had interviewed Wayne 15 years earlier for the book *We All Want to Change the World*. He didn't remember that meeting, until I mentioned that he talked about a TV series he was working on (never made) that would tell the story of sex, drugs, and rock and roll in all its gripping glory, nothing sanitized.

In April 2013, *Rock and Roll Stories* debuted, with Wayne Kramer, former guitarist with the legendary MC5, as the initial guest. My second was Charles Wright, founding member of the Watts 103rd Street Rhythm and Blues Band, the man who wrote the endlessly memorable and perpetually relevant hit "Express Yourself." The connection to Charles had come through David Reyes.

At this point, the show started to gain momentum, with viewers discovering it on their own, since the station did little to promote any of its programs. Within a couple of months, my producer started receiving requests from artists or their management asking to appear as guests. Since I didn't know many rock and roll performers, and neither did he, these referrals were essential to the show's continuing success.

Over the course of 15 months, I interviewed Johnny Rivers, Alan Parsons, Vicki Peterson, Louise Goffin, Lonnie Jordan, Paul Stookey, B.J. Thomas, Mary Gautier, and a number of others tied to the 1960s, 70s, 80s, or 90s. In early 2015, *Rock and Roll Stories* was taken off the air by a different superintendent, who didn't like the idea of his communications director doubling as TV host, regardless of the show's popularity or educational value. My final interview was with the soul crooner Eddie Holman, whose shall we say "healthy ego" provided a fitting, over-the-top sendoff to the program.

I did not receive a cent for the gig—other than my regular school district salary—but I felt like the luckiest person in the world every time I heard the theme music—funky, 1980s-style electric guitar riff—and the teleprompter displayed my opening remarks. For the next 60 minutes, I had no other responsibilities or obligations than hosting a lively conversation with people who had made records that I purchased and listened to for years. It made the other 23 hours of the day seem tepid by comparison.

It was also through *Rock and Roll Stories* that I met the person who would become my collaborator on the first and still only musical I've ever had produced.

One day in the spring of 2014, the show's producer received an e-mail from a songwriter named James Holvay. I was unfamiliar with the name, but in his correspondence Holvay noted that he had written the number one hit (and co-written three other Top 20 hits) by the Buckinghams, a group that had astonishing success in 1967 and early 1968 playing a smooth version of the Blue-eyed soul sound that appealed to Black and white listeners. I had bought a couple of the group's singles at the time, and I recalled that a sixth-grade friend of mine named John bragged about seeing the group in 1968 in Hawaii. He had the photos to prove it.

I invited the personable Holvay to appear on the show, and he shared a number of great stories, including at the age of 10 or 11 receiving a kindly, free, impromptu lesson in how to write songs from blues legend Willie Dixon.

A couple days after the interview, Holvay contacted me about getting together for lunch. I wasn't entirely surprised: We had developed an easygoing repartee on the set, which continued in the greenroom after the cameras went dark. In the course of this wide-ranging conversation, I mentioned to James that I had written the script for a musical based on the rock and roll scene in the Latino communities of Boyle Heights and East Los Angeles during the mid-1960s. He was sufficiently intrigued to want to learn more. I brought two copies to our meeting.

James and I got together at Du-par's Restaurant in Studio City; buoyant, middle-aged waitresses in cute, candy-striped dresses, shiny booths made from soft vinyl, and hearty American cuisine. We could not have selected a more perfect backdrop to discuss the golden ages of rock and roll.

The two of us talked in general about the music business, songs and artists, plus my self-serving list of subjects: *Land of a Thousand Dances: Chicano Rock and Roll from Southern California*, the documentary *Chicano Rock!: The Sounds of East LA* and the encouragement I had received to turn the anecdote about Cannibal and the Headhunters opening for the Beatles at the Hollywood Bowl in 1965 into a full-length, original musical. I noted that the project had initially been attached to a different writer—a veteran practitioner of the form-whose draft I felt did not sufficiently capture the rock and roll fantasy. Rather than look for another author, I impatiently and presumptively spent several months working on the version that was now before us.

"There's just one problem," I explained to James, ignoring the fact that I was a rookie scriptwriter, which could also be considered a barrier, "I don't have a collaborator." I picked up the script. "It's a musical without any music."

"That is a problem," agreed James. He went silent for a few seconds.

"I'm going to read this over, see what I can do," he said. "I have no experience with writing musicals, but you never know…"

(Many months later, when we were far along in the process, James told me that I had perfect timing. He was starting to emerge from a decades-long, self-imposed retreat from anything to do with the music business, a result of trying unsuccessfully for years to make it big with his white soul band, the MOB. If I had approached him even a few months earlier, he most likely would not have volunteered to save *Eastside Heartbeats*, but simply wished me the best.)

I had included in the script the places where it made sense to insert a song, even adding possible titles. I had barely returned home from our lunch when James started sending me e-mails asking what type of sound and pace I envisioned for each of the numbers; ballad, up-tempo rock and roll, mid-1960s soul, folk rock, and so on. He also insisted on receiving lyrics as soon as they were written.

It was quickly apparent to me that my new collaborator was not just eager to write songs, but also willing to help steer this large, unruly ship, a contribution that I had obviously not expected. Before that time, I had felt alone, working on the musical in the company of a small group of people who expressed support and encouragement but didn't want to become fully involved. What a pleasure to finally meet someone who cared about its fate as much as I did. Succeed or fail, we were now collectively bound to the project.

As with writing the script, I had no training—formal or otherwise—in the art of writing lyrics. I was guided purely by arrogance, impatience, and instinct. I had sung lyrics, quoted lyrics, and memorized lyrics; what more did I need to know? I was aware that the words should rhyme, and that they can rhyme line-by-line or every other line. I also had a well-honed, decades-in-the-making bias against sappy or pretentious lyrics; according to my definition, of course.

Relying on my own, well-stocked CD collection, I created an impromptu lesson plan that included the Beatles, Smokey Robinson and the Miracles, the Rolling Stones, Tom Petty, and various clever pop hits. My cobbled together syllabus failed to include show tunes for the simple reason that I didn't own any soundtracks. I justified to myself this obvious omission by noting that *Eastside Heartbeats* was a *rock and roll* musical.

I now needed to understand the utilitarian purpose of lyrics: Not in the "I-get-what-they're-saying" sense, but in the "so-that's-how-they-do-it" sense, lines building on and playing off each other to communicate mood and feeling, which in this case would reveal the characters' inner life and motivations. In the course of my research, I discovered things that I had somehow missed for decades, such as "Norwegian Wood" is one of the few Beatle songs that tell an actual story from beginning to end, like a novel.

Compared to writing pop, rock, or folk lyrics, my job seemed ridiculously easy. Dylan, Lennon, McCartney, Jagger, Smokey Robinson, Springsteen, and the rest took their ideas from everyday life, which was far too much artistic freedom for my limited imagination. I required the structure of a predetermined set of circumstances; character or characters guided by specific actions and feelings.

In fact, once I started working on the script, I recognized rather quickly where songs would neatly fit into the story, better than straight dialogue. The interludes made sense, which was counter to how I had once thought about musicals. *Characters suddenly break out in song to convey their feelings? How absurd*! A form that for years had seemed utterly illogical now struck me as eminently logical.

Despite having a laptop and an iPhone, I wrote the lyrics in pencil on a yellow pad of paper, either stretched out on my bed or slumped in a large leather chair, unconcerned about the effect on my lower back. I needed the space to get up and walk about the room, muttering to myself while trying to find the clever word or sentence to convey a character's thoughts and feelings. I experienced a kind of frantic intensity coming up with the words to songs, not unlike when I had to complete a press release from scratch for a demanding boss in less than 20 minutes.

I would write an initial line, often derived from the working title, and then go through a tortuous process to come up with a second, and so on until the end. The excruciating gap between the initial attempt and its follow-up could last a few minutes to as much as an hour. In the longer instances, I put on full display my melodramatic interpretation of the anguished writer; lie on the floor, assail the gods of creativity, let loose obscenities like a livid football coach embarrassed by his team's awful performance.

On the other hand, coming up with a line that cleverly conveyed a character's predicament and, in the parlance of critics and directors, advanced the story was pure ecstasy. After all, the lines that made it into the final version would be performed in front of an audience, which if I was lucky, would laugh or reflect in all the right places. When I actually experienced these moments, the psychic return on investment was greater than anything I had ever derived from writing a single sentence in a book, an article, or an opinion piece, no matter how "brilliant." I had attended hundreds of plays, but not until I wrote my own script did I ruminate on what it must have been like for Tennessee Williams to first see Blanche Dubois come to life, or for Edward Albee to watch his George and Martha do battle in *Who's Afraid of Virginia Woolf?*. Or, while we're on the subject, what went through Shakespeare's mind when he finally saw Hamlet walk the stage.

I had been told by the original producer of the show — who left before it opened — that composers in the musical theater field invariably perform their songs for the rest of the creative team on piano, unaccompanied. But James, who did not come out of that world, had written hits for the pop and R&B charts and believed wholeheartedly in the power of the studio. For *Eastside Heartbeats*, he hired musicians and a vocalist to record each song. He then sent me by regular mail the completed version on a disk.

James composed at a frenetic pace, taking no more than a few days to complete a new number. He had a singular knack for appropriating sounds of the era, while somehow making them his own and remaining true to the script. "Thank You, Mr. Epstein" sounded like the British group, the Searchers; "They Don't Know Me" had the distinct mood and feel of a Motown ballad; "Don't Know What's

Happening Here," which captured the turmoil and fear associated with the 1965 Watts riots and the seemingly never-ending issue of police brutality, was influenced by the contemplative soul sounds made popular at the end of the 1960s and early 1970s by Marvin Gaye and Curtis Mayfield.

Prior to getting a working draft of the songs and script, I had discovered the ideal performance space. At the very beginning of this journey, I had made the decision to debut *Eastside Heartbeats* in a neighborhood that would be immediately receptive to an original musical that told a story about the transformative effect of soul and rhythm and blues on the Mexican-American community of East Los Angeles and Boyle Heights: A part of town where the local audience would instinctively understand the context, humor, and references.

One Saturday morning in late 2013, I read a positive review in the *Los Angeles Times* about a production of *In the Heights*, Lin-Manuel Miranda's first musical, which centered around a classic American success story within the sprawling Latino community of New York—Cubans, Dominicans, and Puerto Ricans. The show was being performed at a theater called Casa 0101 (Casa), located in Boyle Heights, just a few miles east of my apartment in Downtown Los Angeles. I phoned the box office and reserved two tickets for that evening's performance.

Selecting a theater is not unlike choosing a home, albeit on a smaller scale. The "buyer" considers the aesthetics, the architecture, the exterior and the interior, the accessibility and size of the restrooms, the den (or in this case the lobby) the available parking, and the acoustics. On that basis, I was ready to move into Casa 0101 right away.

The theater was located between a cozy, long-standing Mexican restaurant on one side and a hardware store that had served the community for decades on the other. Its storefront windows, which advertised the current show in words and photos, and mid-sized marquee, had the nostalgic allure of an art house cinema from the 1970s.

The interior of Casa featured a lengthy, thin walkway that contained paintings and photography along one of its walls. I'd attended hundreds of plays, but I could not recall ever being in a community-based theater that doubled as a multimedia art gallery. To step inside Casa was to be instantly enveloped by the local culture, a vibrant, historic neighborhood depicted in vivid colors and shapes.

The stage had the musty and fussy feel of an active rehearsal room, with props and other theater paraphernalia stored to the sides. There was no curtain; the actors entered and exited through narrow passageways at the back. Though not large, the performance space was of sufficient size to accommodate a modest musical, perhaps 10 or 12 dancers could move without stepping on and over each other. Stairs on either side led to a narrow, stage-length catwalk on which actors could perform or wait in the shadows. With its feeling of impermanence, the Casa space was a set designer's dream, ripe for reinvention with each new play or musical.

The theater had room for 99 patrons, in strict accordance with Equity rules. The rows were sloped, which meant the audience was looking down at the performance, from a not-uncomfortable angle.

The production of *In the Heights* was exuberant and colorful, a splashy love letter to Latin New York. Well before the actors made their final bows to the audience, I knew that this was the theater for *Eastside Heartbeats*—an ode to Latino LA.

During the week between Christmas and New Year's 2013 I called Casa, on a whim, not thinking that theater people like the rest of us often go on vacation at the end of the calendar year.

Not only did someone answer the phone at Casa that December 27, it was the executive director himself, Emmanuel Deleage. No answering machine, no intern assigned to the phones while upper management enjoyed its time away. I introduced myself, and abruptly went into pitch mode, giving a quick synopsis of the plot and the characters, finishing with why this show would be ideal for that venue. I did the entire presentation in fifteen breathless minutes. At the end Emmanuel was sufficiently intrigued, inviting me to meet him at the space for a tour, after the first of the year.

I brought along the original producer and music director, both of whom were no longer part of the team when *Eastside Heartbeats* opened in January 2016. Like me, they recognized Casa's geographic and theatrical advantages. Emmanuel checked the schedule and indicated that there was a five-week gap in the fall when the show could be slotted. I was a little disappointed; 10 months or more was a long time to wait, even if I was in need of a songwriter. But that was just me being greedy. We now had a venue, which was what mattered most.

As we were leaving, Emmanuel raised the subject of funding. In my naiveté, I had assumed that his theater or any theater simply paid for productions out of its own budget. Emmanuel smiled and explained it's not quite that simple. He said many enthusiastic creators bring worthy projects to Casa, only to be defeated by lack of money. These shows, he explained in a sober tone, never make it past a stage reading.

Emmanuel went into detail about rental and other costs associated with a production of this type. He said Casa might perhaps offer a break here or there, but the actual raising of funds would be our responsibility. Securing financing for a community theater production can be as daunting a prospect as lining up the capital for a Hollywood blockbuster. Whether we're talking $10,000 or $100,000,000, without the money the show can't go on.

Move forward 18 months, the summer of 2015. I brought in a new producer, my well-connected friend Maria Elena Yepes, who was in the process of forming her own company, Brown Fist Productions. Maria Elena had spent decades at East Los Angeles Community College, and she knew many Latino community, cultural, and political leaders. In a matter of a few frenzied months, Maria Elena managed to raise the funds — almost exclusively from government and nonprofit coffers — to support a four-week run. Once the financing was in place, Emmanuel added us to the Casa schedule for January and February 2016.

Once word got out in the summer and early fall of 2015 about the musical, a couple of veterans of the Chicano rock and roll scene in Los Angeles who had claimed exclusive rights to the "Cannibal and the Headhunters" name and story made threatening noises about initiating legal action. I carried on a periodic conversation with one of them, who in the end decided not to take us to court, for reasons that were not entirely clear. Although I and the rest of the team were confident that we would prevail, a lawsuit would have effectively shut down *Eastside Heartbeats*. We barely had enough money to launch the show, let alone hire an attorney.

(The guy who issued the threat never attended the production. Oh well, his loss.)

In the six months before *Eastside Heartbeats* opened, and after the show was up and running, James and the rest of the production team did much of our critical work at a Denny's restaurant located just behind Union Station in downtown Los Angeles, within walking distance of my apartment. I liked the vegetable omelets, at any time of day, and James preferred the steak or fish dinners. We were also drawn to the spot because the sound system played nothing but rock and roll and rhythm and blues from the mid-1950s to the end of the 1960s. Here we were fine-tuning a show about the East LA music scene circa 1965 while hearing above us many of the same songs that our characters would have listened to as teenagers. In gratitude, James christened the establishment "Rock and Roll Denny's."

We got lucky with the auditions. Though Los Angeles is a city filled with actors, comparatively few of them are young Latino guys with a burning desire to perform in musicals. We saw a total of six people for the four young men who make up the Eastside Heartbeats. Still, if the director and I had auditioned 50 candidates, the quartet we selected would have been at or near to the top of the list.

Brimming with enthusiasm and charm, agile, and great-looking, this unit became the Heartbeats early in the rehearsal process, and the bond only grew stronger over time. After many shows, young girls would gather around the individual "members," offer compliments along the lines of "You were so great" and politely request autographs. In those moments, I allowed myself the fantasy that we captured Beatlemania in a bottle.

The full cast did a table read the Sunday after Thanksgiving, 2015, and rehearsals began the next day. At the time I was working as a communications consultant for Caltech, a 6-month gig that I took on after departing the Los Angeles Unified School District at the end of June 2015. Caltech never knew what to do with me, and I never knew what to do with Caltech. The days passed slowly, especially after the perpetual spotlight and high drama of the school district. I spent much of my time monitoring press coverage for a world-class research center with brilliant students and faculty, right next door but out of my reach.

Although I worked humane hours — 9 a.m. to 5 p.m. with rare exceptions— and I had an easy six-mile commute against traffic, I invariably felt tired and rather listless when I got home. By 10 pm, I was in bed, hoping for a restful sleep before doing it all over again.

When I arrived back at my apartment after the first night of rehearsal, I was my usual low-grade self, consuming my usual microwave organic meal for dinner. But instead of the customary early evening options — turning on the television, reading *The New Yorker* or a book — after I finished I drove to Casa, 10 minutes away.

I had not attended a musical theater rehearsal in 47 years, sixth grade to be precise, when I was cast as Jack in the John Muir Elementary School production of *Puss and Boots*. Mary, the girl I was in love with at the time, played Dorothea, who happened to be Jack's romantic interest: Art imitating life, and we were only in the sixth grade. Aside from the fortuitous casting, however, I don't remember a single moment of the rehearsal process. I do remember that for her costume Mary wore an Elizabethan-style purple dress with puffy sleeves, and after the performance she told me "You were great, Tom," and I told her she was great, too.

I didn't expect such excitement this time around; at least from me, well on my way to 60. When I got to the theater, the director, Corky Dominguez, was working with a small group of actors, breaking down the characters and story. The music director, Gary St. Germain, and the vocal coach, Melodee Fernandez, were going over some of the songs with a different set of performers. I took a seat in the middle row and watched all of it, without making comments or taking notes. From the start, I was cognizant of not wanting to be the interventionist playwright; adding my own perspective without solicitation and potentially undercutting the creative team.

Being asked for my opinion was another matter, however. Corky periodically called on me, and I always took the opportunity to share my thoughts. It was quite collegial, differences in interpretation handled with tact and friendly concessions, no screaming scenes. On my end, some of this was strategic. Angry rows while the actors were present struck me as the theatrical equivalent of parents fighting in front of the children; a prospect to be avoided, if at all possible, for the bad example it sets and the dispiriting, depressing effect it has on impressionable witnesses.

By the third rehearsal, Corky asked me to read lines with various actors, which I found to be exhilarating. To that point, this collection of characters — male and female, young and early middle-age, nearly all of them Latino — had existed only in the head of a white male in his late fifties.

The first time at rehearsal that the Chilean actress Bernardita Nassar, or "Bernie," performed the entire song "Selling Out," a Holvay/Waldman composition, with Gary St. Germain accompanying her on solo piano, was my greatest thrill ever in theater, as an audience member or participant. In her street clothes, with actors and tech hands milling about, Bernie sang the number as if it was opening night, applying an exquisite, soaring tone and emotive finish, achieved without any direction.

I cherished going to rehearsal; even found the drudge work — blocking, routine stage notes — fresh and exciting. I would arrive at Casa tired from another typical day at Caltech, and yet 15 minutes later, I felt like I could last until at least 3 a.m. without a single break. I was perpetually disappointed when 11 p.m. came, the time to quit for the evening, per theater rules. When I arrived home, it would be another hour at least before I could get into bed, let alone fall asleep. This new schedule was not conducive to starting my day job refreshed and ready to go, but I was more than willing to make the sacrifice.

I am not a spiritual person, but it felt during this period like I was having a religious experience, except that instead of Jesus or Buddha, I had given over my heart, mind, and soul to the god of musical theater. Even the mundane manifestations of everyday life suddenly pulsed with excitement. I had always mocked the idea that existence can be beautiful, and now I here was behaving like a toddler who had just learned how to walk.

The dress rehearsal took place on a Thursday night, 24 hours before the official opening. David Reyes had assembled a live band to accompany the songs, which included Holvay on rhythm guitar, three young guys playing lead guitar, bass, and drums, and Gary on keyboards, also acting as music director. They were positioned in a pit to the right of the stage, visible but not distractingly so.

The final dress rehearsal went quite well, no mistakes were made that could be noticed by anyone outside of the insiders, enthusiasm and dedication were on full display. The cast was not just as ready as they would ever be for opening night, they were ready, period. Afterwards, the creative team sat around with the Casa folks and analyzed the performance. Josefina Lopez, the well-known Chicana playwright and founding artistic director of Casa, got teary-eyed talking about the story. The unanimous view from the invited audience was that *Eastside Heartbeats* would have a highly successful run!

I drove my friend, Ira, who had attended the performance from Boyle Heights to Universal City, where his car was parked at the subway station, then turned around and headed back downtown. During the entire return trip, I was in a state of ecstasy, having achieved a dream that was not so much impossible as unimaginable. I attended many musicals, but had not once fantasized about being an actor, director, or writer. For 40 years, I was just an audience member, or occasionally the critic. And now, at age 59, I was making my debut on the American stage, in a manner of speaking. You're never too old to be young.

Eastside Heartbeats sold out every night of its run in January and February. About halfway through, Emmanuel told me that a musical scheduled for May had been forced to cancel, and he asked if we would like to take its place. Yes, I said, without hesitation, before consulting the other members of the team, who I knew would agree.

For this second run we hired a publicist, who secured a major feature story in the Sunday entertainment section of the *Los Angeles Times*, plus articles in smaller publications and a TV segment on the 11 p.m. news. A number of rock and roll people attended the show, including Vicki Peterson from the Bangles, Chris Montez, and the one surviving member of Cannibal and the Headhunters, who flew in from Tucson and cried during and after the performance. A few of the cast members from January/February departed prior to May, but we were able to find talented replacements.

I attended nearly all the performances during both the first and the second productions. For most of the shows, I sat in the booth at the top of theater, in cramped quarters next to the stage manager and his assistant. It was the perfect location to surreptitiously watch the reactions from members of the audience, who were obviously not looking at me. I could not only tell when they laughed, but how much they laughed, which was admittedly a gauge I used purely for ego purposes.

More important, I could determine when attendees seemed bored and fidgety, a sign to me that the show dragged, especially if it was during the same places night after night. It was partly on the basis of these reactions that we decided to cut lines of dialogue and one number from the second production. Not an easy decision, but I would rather sacrifice a song and some words than see disengaged theatergoers checking their watches.

By the time it closed at the end of May, *Eastside Heartbeats* had exceeded even our ambitious projections. On the strength of our obvious success, I figured musical theater diehards with impressive bank accounts would take us to the next level, a venue in Hollywood, the Westside, or a major city outside Los Angeles. There was just one big problem; we didn't know those people, and the people who told us they did know those people, either also didn't know these people or couldn't get them to provide funding. As of this writing, James and I are hoping to renew our efforts now that theaters are reopening safely.

When I get too down about the future prospects for *Eastside Heartbeats*, I remind myself that the musical would never have happened had I not overseen the school district's public television station, my nervy suggestion that I be allowed to create and host a rock and roll show, and my chance meeting and subsequent friendship with a guest who essentially booked himself on the program. It makes me feel better every time.

CHAPTER 24 (BONUS TRACK II)

"Good Night"

The Beatles, 1968

I happened to be working at Tower Records during the first stirrings of rap and hip hop. In late 1979, some outfit called the Sugarhill Gang released a 12-inch single called "Rapper's Delight." The forward-thinking person in charge of "dance music" — a category that had evolved from disco — ordered hundreds of copies, which we stacked near the front cash register, certain to get noticed. At least once per day, an employee played the song over the store's sound system; our modest contribution to what would become a revolution in American popular music.

The torrent of words — an audacious, wacky autobiography — resembled nothing I could recall except for select lines from a few Bob Dylan songs from the mid-1960s. Still, that wasn't the craziest part. The entire, seven-minute track was beat for beat, note for note, and riff for riff "Good Times" by Chic, which had gone to #1 only the year before. How did the Sugarhill Gang, whoever they were, expect to get away with that?

I was 23 at the time—getting up there in pop years, though still young enough to appreciate new sounds—yet I wondered when lawyers would come after "Rapper's Delight." Although I didn't know much about copyright law, it seemed evident to me that one song couldn't blatantly steal the recognizable elements of another song without legal consequences. Otherwise, why didn't white pop groups in the 1960s simply copy the Beatles note for note and enjoy the rewards?

No kidding, I fully anticipated that men in trench coats would enter my Tower Records and thousands of other stores around the country to abscond with every remaining copy of "Rapper's Delight." In my scenario, which had echoes of a police state, the single would be confiscated and then destroyed; a cautionary tale for any slick producers in the future who wanted to foist a blatant fraud on the public.

As any music fan knows, however, "Rapper's Delight" did not disappear from the shelves. (I do recall some legal bustle around the song, but nothing to cause it to be removed from Tower or any other record store.) Instead, this unlikely hit launched a sound and style that has dominated pop tastes for more than four decades, with no signs of abating. Over that time, rap and hip hop, which came from the streets, has generated billions of dollars, more than enough to enlist the priciest law firms against charges of plagiarism.

Like rock in the 1960s, rap and hip hop has been studied and written about by the intellectual elite and is part of the course curriculum at many academic institutions around the country. Of all the predictions I've made in my lifetime, rap and hip hop's eventual demise was among the worst, right there with 24-hour news channels will make us smarter, better-informed citizens.

Little more than a year after the release of "Rapper's Delight," I left Tower to concentrate on building a career in journalism. I was now 24, and I would never again be as closely connected to new trends in pop music. My current CD collection includes some prominent groups from the 1990s and 2000s — including Oasis, Smashmouth, the Raconteurs, the Vines, and the Decembrists — but I heard these artists by accident, rather than as part of a deliberate quest for exciting sounds. I am also an enthusiastic consumer of documentaries on Taylor Swift, Ariana Grande, and other extraordinary female performers from the 2010s and 2020s. It is a source of continual fascination to me how the top musicians of any generation build and sustain their incredibly successful careers.

When I embraced the Monkees back in the fall of 1966, I was not seeking entry into the heretofore unexplored world of pop music. I simply liked what I heard, and wanted to hear more of it, from them, exclusively. But within a few months, my tastes had expanded well beyond these four guys who appeared on my TV every Monday night. By 1968, I was actively listening to performers who did not match the typical profile of a Caucasian kid raised in a virtually all-white suburb: Marvin Gaye, the Temptations, James Brown, Curtis Mayfield, Sam and Dave, the Isley Brothers.

I had help in this area. My interest in soul and funk was the direct result of having attended an integrated junior high school in Berkeley from 1968–1969. The exposure to different artists that resulted from my sharing the campus with Black students changed how I listened to and assessed popular music. I started devoting a portion of my severely limited entertainment budget to soul and rhythm and blues, along with rock. In early 1969, I purchased the single of "I Heard it Through the Grapevine," adding it to the very few 45s in my collection.

After our family returned to Claremont, I started buying many more soul and funk singles for around $1 dollar each at the local Singer Sewing Machine store. My interest in these genres had not diminished, even though the Black student population at my new school was no more than 5–7%. I also embraced artists whom I had never heard in Berkeley, such as Southern California's own Brenton Wood, whose 1967 hit, "The Oogum Boogum Song," I frantically pursued across the AM dial.

During my four years at Claremont High School, I never met a white kid who listened to or liked Brenton Wood. I did have some close white friends at CHS who thought it was absurd that I listened to, and liked, Brenton Wood. But in pop music and life, what doesn't kill me makes me stronger. I defiantly played Brenton Wood singles, and if the others objected, on whatever idiotic grounds, they were free to leave the room.

I didn't learn for another decade that Brenton Wood was hugely popular with the Latino community across the region, making a very good living performing at venues in cities with majority Latino populations. It turned out that I wasn't alone after all.

In the early 1990s, I had the opportunity to interview Mr. Wood as part of my research for *Land of a Thousand Dances: Chicano Rock and Roll from Southern California*. We met for a couple of hours in a nearly deserted, aging Chinese restaurant in the northeast San Fernando Valley. To that point, the flesh-and-blood Brenton Wood had been elusive to me, a person I had seen for no more than a few seconds during a local television appearance in the early 1970s. And now the magisterial voice that gave the world "Me and You," "Baby You Got It," and "The Oogum Boogum Song" was talking about his entire career while speaking into my tape recorder. I rank it alongside sitting down with Peter Tork as my greatest thrill in music journalism.

In an ideal world, our musical choices — classical, jazz, Top 40 — should be private and personal. If we are lucky enough to be exposed to other forms, especially at a reasonably young age, or sufficiently open-minded to do the exploring on our own, we are better able to make the decisions that work for us. We should avoid making these decisions under pressure, which is not always possible. After all, there is a social price to pay for pursuing one's own taste, as I discovered, and so did that Black kid named James who brought *Revolver* to our first period music class at Willard Junior High School in 1969. It can be threatening to the upholders of "majority" culture; however, that's defined — when someone who apparently should know better deviates from the script.

In some instances, I opted to remain in the musical closet rather than subject myself to teasing and taunts. Even by the liberal standards of the decade, Pitzer College in 1975–1976 was the epitome of cultural tolerance, at least on the surface: easy availability of magic mushrooms; guilt-free, casual sex; a surplus of open, proud lesbians; and more witches and warlocks than I could count. Still, it did not feel like a safe space for me to play my Doo Wop music, much of it having originated in the despised 1950s, the infamous decade of oppressive gender roles, mindless anticommunism, and neurotic double lives. In this heady environment of multipronged liberation, what would it say about me as a political, social, cultural entity if I listened to and loved songs that represented an era that was finally, joyously being dismantled?

As a result, I elected to keep the volume turned way down on my bedside radio. I was not prepared to sacrifice what little standing I had within the Pitzer community to openly broadcast my love of dreamy romantic ballads from the era of going steady. It was easier and safer to keep my forbidden passion to myself. If that made me a cultural coward, so be it. In my three years at Pitzer, no one but a few close, trustworthy friends ever knew that I adored Doo Wop.

In this book, I have attempted to demonstrate how my pop music choices offered a parallel history of my own personal experiences, as seen through the high drama of post-World War II American life. In my case, it was driven by rock and roll and rhythm and blues, but for another person the catalyst could just as well have been film, theater, television, or the visual arts. I happened to get a visceral charge from rock that carried over into other aspects of my life, without my consciously seeking that link.

I eventually found my crowd, quite by accident, and it cut across educational, ethnic, racial, class, and in some cases chronological lines. I also discovered that a common passion for culture can be the basis for the strongest friendships, even more so than politics or sports. Long after *Eastside Heartbeats* closed, James Holvay and I have continued to gather at Rock and Roll Denny's, where we spend hours talking about records and artists. There are few things in life that compare with the sheer bliss of these conversations. They don't so much end as fade out, like my favorite songs.

In my teens and 20s, I considered pop music to be both a welcome diversion and essential. I was madly in love with the whole industry — albums, singles, magazines, books, fashions — but I also had to make a living. The idea of combing the two never seriously occurred to me. To this day, I am in awe of the men and women who found a way to bust into the system, not only as musicians, but as journalists, photographers, publicists, and managers. I am as eager to read their memoirs as I am those of the rock stars they followed and worked for. The two volumes of Rolling Stones' manager/producer Andrew Loog Oldham's oral history of the English rock scene in the 1960s, along with music journalist Nick Kent's *Apathy for the Devil*, a vivid portrait of the English rock scene in the 1970s, are as good or better than 99% of the books about those astonishing periods in pop music.

And yet, I found a way to cross the line from fan to observer to participant, which could not have been predicted in my craziest fantasies. Even better, it was the culmination of a cultural and sociological journey that began in my early 20s, when I first became aware that the music I listened to entirely on my own was also hugely popular with the Mexican-American community in Southern California. Until that point, I was woefully ignorant of this connection, despite living in a county with the name "Los Angeles" and growing up near cities with sizeable Latino populations.

Through a purely selfish reason — shared love of ballads — I was inspired to learn more about the Latino community of Southern California; culture, politics, economics, demographics, and sociology. I am no expert, not even close, but even my limited understanding would not have been possible without the rhythm and blues introduction.

I carried this knowledge inside me when I wrote the script for *Eastside Heartbeats*. I would have never attempted to tell the story of a Mexican-American vocal group from the 1960s without the anecdotal evidence and firsthand experiences to back it up. My immersion in pop music — beginning with the Monkees — had in some marvelous, mysterious way brought me to a point nearly 50 years later where I was writing the book and lyrics for a musical about a vocal quartet of ambitious teenagers from Boyle Heights, who were immersed in the scene around the same time I was going mad for "Last Train to Clarksville." My musical was based on an extended anecdote I first heard while working with David Reyes on the book *Land of a Thousand Dances: Chicano Rock and Roll from Southern California.*

*   *   *

I used to think there was something wrong with the millions of people who liked pop music but didn't see it as essential to existence. I have since made the wise and mature decision to withhold judgment and let them be who they are. Still, I can't conceive of being alive at any time in the entire history of humankind without the benefit of rock and roll, R&B, funk, punk, and disco. This book is a tribute to my good fortune.

THE END

ABOUT THE AUTHOR

Tom Waldman is co-author of *Land of a Thousand Dances: Chicano Rock'n'Roll From Southern California*, the most comprehensive look at the flourishing Latino rock and roll scene from Ritchie Valens through Los Lobos. He was also creator and host of the television program *Rock and Roll Stories*, which aired on KLCS, the PBS station in Los Angeles, from 2013–2015. His guests included Wayne Kramer, Johnny Rivers, Vicki Peterson, B.J. Thomas, Louise Goffin, Alan Parsons, and James Holvay. In 2016 Tom wrote the script for the original musical, *Eastside Heartbeats*, which was staged and sold out for eight weeks at Casa 0101 Theatre in Los Angeles' Boyle Heights neighborhood. The show is a fictional rendition of the true story of the Mexican-American vocal group Cannibal and the Headhunters, whose fame first stemmed for being the group who opened for the Beatles at the Hollywood Bowl in August 1965. Presently, Tom continues researching and writing about the musical genres he loves most from his home in Los Angeles.

INDEX